INTELLIGIBLE LIFE

BY

ALLAMEH M. T. JAFARI

TRANSLATED FROM ORIGINAL PERSIAN INTO

ENGLISH BY: BEYTOLLAH NADERLEW

EDITED BY: SEEMA ARIF

Top Ten Award International Network
Vancouver, BC
Canada

Published by: Top Ten Award International Network Inc.

Vancouver, BC **CANADA**
Email: Info@TopTenAward.Net
www.toptenaward.net

Ordering Information:
Quantity sales. Special discounts are available on quantity purchases by universities, schools, corporations, associations, and others. For details, contact the "Sales Department" at the above mentioned email address.

Intelligible Life, 'Allamah Muhammad Taqi Ja'fari
ISBN: 978-1-990451-90-4   Paperback

In The Name Of Allah, the most Beneficent, the most Gracious, the most Merciful!

Allameh Muhammad Taghi Jafari

(1923-1998)

Contents

Acknowledgements

This project would not have been possible without the valuable support and time given by many people. We are deeply indebted to everyone for their contribution as well as moral support. We are grateful to Professor Seyed G. Safavi from London Academy of Iranian Studies, University of London, UK for his personal interest and motivation for this project to introduce Allama's work at international level in a comparative context. The project has been possible by assiduous effort of Beytollah Naderlew, who took the responsibility of translating it into English. We are obliged by Professor Seyed Farid al-Attas from National University of Singapore for his well-researched and thought-provoking epilogue for the book, providing a real time context of comparative Islamic intellectual discourse on Alternative Sociology. We would like to offer special thanks to Professor Seema Arif from The University of Central Punjab, Lahore, Pakistan, who undertook the responsibility of editing this work. We would also like to thank Ms. Roya Azizi Mousavi for setting its computer layout, and Mr. Saeed Ajami for designing the cover of this book.

The Allameh Jafari Institute

About the Author

Allama Muhammad Taghi Jafari (1923-1998), was born in a religious family in Tabriz, Iran. His parents were pious and greatly respected by the community. Allama started formal schooling from the 4th grade as he was taught reading and writing by his mother at home. Allama's formal religious education began at the Talebieh seminary in Tabriz, where he grew to become an outstanding student of Ayatollah Shahidi. He had also studied under the celebrated teachers of his time in Tehran and Qom for a while, but his real mentor advised him to attend Najaf School of Theology, where he stayed for 11 years. He made remarkable progress and was awarded the highest degree of jurisprudence – Ijthad – at the young age of 23. After completing his education, he began teaching in Najaf.

Allama Jafari is the contemporary sage who has expounded his theory about Sociology of Islam. His domain of interest includes practical issues and problems faced by people in social living. He is an original and innovative thinker in providing genuine solutions being well versed in Islamic Fiqh, methods of Western philosophy, and knowledge as it is advanced by social sciences. He has continued the tradition of great masters like Allama Tabatabaei, martyr Ayatollah Seyed Muhammad Bagher Sadr, and martyr Ayatollah Motahari to bring classical Islamic knowledge in modern diction to quench the thirst of youth with eternal spring of original knowledge. To realize the mission, the honorable master Allama Muhammad Taghi Jafari has made innovative use of knowledge extracted from modern disciplines like psychology, sociology, anthropology, and political science by rationalizing it in context of classic Muslim Philosophy and ethics as coded in Nahj-al-balaqeh, Mathnavi Maulana Rumi and other great works.

His voluminous work speaks unconditionally of the rejuvenation of rational thought in Islam. He offers us a broad range of topics and issues related to human needs and basic rights discussed in various paradigms, such as Arts, Humanities, Philosophy, Aesthetics, Literature, Mysticism, Psychology and Pedagogy. In spite of being a devoted scholar of Muslim philosophy and Master of Fiqh (jurisprudence), he did not ignore the invaluable wealth of wisdom replete in Islamic mysticism. Allama had fully realized the powerful impact of classical Greek thought in renaissance of European World. He knew how to dive deep for pearls of wisdom in works of ancient philosophers such as Socrates, Plato, and Aristotle as well as modern, e.g. Descartes, Leibniz, Hume, Kant and Hegel. His great appetite for knowledge also relished the taste of world literature such as Balzac, Dostoevsky, Tolstoy, Hugo, and modern-day physicists including Max Planck, and Einstein. He says:

> *"The true intellectual should always maintain his contact with the vast sea of knowledge in the flow of time, and make use of current logics, known cause-and-effects and their impacts tactfully to make intelligible life in his society a reality. It is mandatory to feel personal obligation and do one's duty by taking any number of suitable measures to realize one's mission."*

His contemporaries remember him as a man who "never rejected anyone; Allama Jafari was a teacher, not a judge!" His passion was to unveil the unknown about the phenomenon of human life. "Life," he believed, "should always be inspired by the original and must follow originality, or it would be merely a burden on man's shoulders." He can be called the philosopher of life, for most of his intellectual pursuits involved knowing about relationship between man and society. He had believed that "Beyond their appearance, all human cultures have a lot in common, and are inseparably associated." He was in search of that unitary element that devises "common human culture" and was able to present it in uniform styles of life that are observed in all societies and cultures: the 'natural' lifestyle and the 'intelligible' one.

Allama Jafari had shared long and intimate friendship with his contemporaries Muhammad Reza Muzaffar, the great philosopher, and Ahmad Amin, the renowned mathematician of Baghdad University and author of the book At-takamol fil-Islam (Evolution in Islam). Allama had a great taste for modern social sciences, and he began his research work with open minded skepticism. Allama Jafari strongly believed in originality and discussion. Those who knew him well and had witnessed his long years of study and research would admit that nothing was more important to him than asking and answering questions. He often shifted from one field of science to another in search of answers to questions and spent most of his time reading books that contained new scientific material and ideas, which provided him with new questions. He said:

> "Questions actually mean that the questioner is saying that he has encountered a dark point on his path toward knowledge, and is eager to overcome it. Thus, passing the bridges and turns of doubt that are the necessity of the phenomenon we call asking, is quite natural. In fact, we can say that on the long road to knowledge, the more bridges and turns we pass with certainty, the better. That means facing many questions."

Allama's epistemic geometry comprises of the knowledge of the mind, the revelation of the heart, of tradition and modernity, physics and metaphysics, and the law and aesthetics. While the first three sources were the main pillars of his thinking, still the expressions of his thoughts were the result of a dialogue among the different basis of this epistemic geometry, which for its up-to-date research and dialogue, made his works novel and attentive to the debates on the issues and problems faced by the "modern human" in the "modern life".

His first book, The Relationship between Man and the Universe, shows the enthusiasm of a young scholar in pursuit of knowledge as well as his firm faith and fortitude in principles of Islam. Allama has strongly believed that man and the universe have objectives and attainable goals and these goals are far higher than man's material pleasures and worldly desires. He has explained his theories based upon "the four relationships" and "the six questions." His six basic questions are: Who am I? Where have I come from? Where have I come to? Who am I with? Why am I here? And where do I go from here? Allama would never leave mankind to drown in his "what there is;" he always called man to "what there should be." Looking for moral excellence, he seeks his ideal values and behaviors in Imam Ali (RA) regarding him as the best proof of four relationships (1-Man-himself, 2-Man-God, 3-Man-the universe, 4- Man-his fellow humans).

"Commentary, Review and Analysis of Rumi's Mathnawi" in fifteen volumes and "Translation and Interpretation of the Nahj-al-balaqeh" in twenty seven volumes have a distinct place in Allama's body of work. Referring to the first, Professor Nasr has noted in the foreword he wrote for "The Structure of Rumi's Mathnawi" written by Professor Safavi (Safavi, S. G., 2006), "it allowed for the tradition of writing commentary on Mathnawi-Manavi, from Mulla Hadi Sabzevari to Allama Jafari, to endure." Moreover, when Allama took the challenge of writing commentaries on these two noble texts, one of which is rendered "the Quran in Persian" by Jami and the other is the immortal work of the Master of Masters, Imam Ali (RA), both the texts were considered obsolete in intellectual circles of seminaries as well as universities. Clergies would hesitate to talk about of Mathnawi in fear of heresy, and writing commentaries on Nahj-al-Balaghehwas considered a virtue not a science. Scholarship was, and still is seen as footnoting on important books of fiqh (jurisprudence). It was in such an environment that the honorable master unveiled the beauty of Mathnawi, restoring its worth and esteem in the creative minds of students and scholars.

By comparing Rumi's sublime and amorous assertions with those of French and Russian thinkers and scholars, with whom modern Iranian intellectuals are more familiar, he reintroduced Mathnawi to Iranians who were acquainted with the Western thought and culture only. Afterwards, by writing an exegesis on Nahj-al-balaqeh, "A Manifesto on Wisdom, Mysticism and Politics" he familiarized the younger generation with Islam as religion which is devoid of superstition, factionalism and backwardness, an Islam based on the appropriation of mind, revelation, justice, and love. We deem Allama as the revivalist of the spirit of the Ummah by role playing the vanguard of spiritual assets of Islam, Mathnawi and Nahj-al-balageh. Not only contemporary scholars will benefit from this beacon of light but the future generations will continue seeking illumination through this valuable resource.

According to Allama Jafari, the spirit of love and creativity of mind are the two wings that make humans fly towards the absolute truth. The mind and revelation, science and religion, the mind and sharia (Islamic law) are all compatible and do not contradict one another. Of course, the mind is the solid pillar of knowing (episteme). His political vision renders justice, compassion, mercy, tolerance, serving the people, reliance on consultation (Shura) and shared decision making as the founding pillars of Islamic governance.

Allama was genuinely a humble and modest person, sound in character, and gentle in mannerism. Despite his high stature, he has always kept a low profile, neither exaggerating nor exhibiting traces of arrogance and contemptuousness for others.

He has completely devoted himself for the cultivation of rational thought in Muslims preparing them to get into intelligible life. "Intelligible Life" has been authored based on the ideas that Allama Jafari has dealt with in the 8th volume of 27-volume Translation and interpretation of the Nahj-al-Balagheh. These ideas mainly belong to the fifth decade of Allama's intellectual life. This treatise has been edited and published by The Allama Jafari Institute, Tehran in 2008.

The Allameh Jafari Institute
Feb. 2011

Translator's Note

We are only going to set you straight on the track, if your carriage stands on the rails crookedly; driving is something we shall leave you to do by yourself.

Ludwig Wittgenstein
MS 117 237: 6.3.1940

Drawing on Wittgenstein I want to summarize Jafarian project of **Intelligible Life** by saying that it is to redraft reality both objectively and subjectively. The discourse is drawn on both Platonic and postmodern ideas, seeking a *fundamental* ontology a la Heidegger to paint the Truth in a new collage. The reader will experience a genuine *primordial* perspective of *Life*.

This translation is genuinely an initiative of The Allameh Jafari Institute. I am personally indebted to it for being supportive during the preparation of this translation. By getting involved in this project with it, I've truly realized the importance of Allama Jafari's ideas and the essential need of placing these in the global discourse of knowledge. Allama's high ideals have reincarnated the vision for my personal life, and it will stay with me forever. I wish the same for the readers of this book.

Professor Seema Arif has generously accepted to edit my translation. The reader will experience her wisdom in every line of the book. Her footnotes and glosses will help the reader to keep the right trek of Allama's footsteps. I am very grateful to her. My family and friends have supported me very kindly during the whole project. I don't know how I could compensate everyone's continuous support by simply saying thank you.

I would like to dedicate my efforts to my beloved wife Dr. Sedigheh Moosazadeh Nalband whose unconditional love, support, and trust in me has made this project possible and to whom I return after God for solace and happiness in life.

Beytollah Naderlew
27-07-2011
Zanjan, Iran

Editor's Note

Happily, I have completed the project of editing "Intelligible Life", a remarkable book written by Allama Muhammad Taghi Jafari to explore the essence of life, the scope of our rationality, which will lead us to meet Al-Haq – the Ultimate Truth. I am most pleased to do this project because the subject matter of the book is not about human divide, but human unity and while dealing with the subject Allama transcends above all sectarian languages that divide the whole of humanity and speaks in universal language of human consciousness. Seeking guidance from spiritual mentor Maulana Jalal ud Din Muhammad Rumi he has described the case of weakening human spirit, which is emaciated and have hollowed from inside. No wonder it moans and wails in the tunes of Rumi: "Bishno az nay chun hikayat me kunad,. Az judayi ha shikayat me kunad…!

Intelligible life has addressed the eternal question which has puzzled humankind for ages, which life is more important: life of body or life of mind? Why earthly life is so lowly and why it does not lead to desired consequences? Why do our dreams remain our wishes, and every destination we seek in despondence becomes a mirage to continue with yet another search? What has happened to our senses that our brains are fused, and minds do not illuminate? Is it due to fatigue or boredom resulting from overindulgence with life of natural pleasures or fear and anxiety about failure for life hereafter? Simply, why don't we admit that despite all the intellectual development we boast of, we have forgotten to choose wisely!

Nature has granted the special gift to humankind – the mind. Many animals have brains, but no mind and thus no consciousness of life. They live life swinging amid pleasures and pains, having no control over the movement, direction and speed of the swing and that is also true for many human beings. Sometimes the life is a roller coaster ride, for some it is a merry-go- round, and for others it is like an old and worn out, dead slow swing hanging in the backyard, which squeaks more than moving forward, and it is always pushed back no matter how hard you were trying. For some it is not even swing but a cradle, as Allama has discussed on page (93). The objection that he has raised is that the hand that rocks the cradle – Mother Nature – cannot be so cruel and so selfish that it will turn the cradle into cage for us, never letting us grow out of it? So, what is restricting us? Is it our own selfish dependence upon the safe and known environment, or there is labyrinth spread all around us and glass ceiling up us, or we are born lame, blind, deaf, or dumb?

Here comes the question of free will but I deem it related with perception more. If we perceive there is free will, we will try to execute it and after some trial and error we may learn to use it, master it and command it; but if we perceive otherwise, we feel suffocated, doomed to death and disaster. Can we safely assume here that consciousness depends upon activation of perception, and not merely on sensation, i.e. use of five senses to gain information about the surrounding environment. All of us have the same apparatus, senses and brain, yet the use is unique and different, i.e. of mind. It is just like having a fancy car in your garage, but not knowing how to drive. We will be either dependent on someone who may pity us and take us to the desired ride or we will need to hire a permanent driver; but in both cases, the chances of manipulation increase: What if none has mercy upon us or he/she doesn't want to take us to our desired destination; in the other case, the driver might be ignorant of the way that leads to our desired destination. Despite having the car and the driver, therefore, we might get lost on the way. The same is true for all individuals, societies and nations, who cannot move for some reasons, have reached wrong destinations, or are still lost on the way. It does remind me of the opening chapter of Quran – Al-Fatiha – where we seek refuge of the Merciful that we may not get lost on the way. If that way connects the world on one hand to hell and on the other to heaven, and we are stuck at cross roads, definitely we will search for a conscious way to heaven and would not like to suffer from undue loss in ignorance.

Intelligible Life guides us at every point to walk on the right path, live and die like a believer, have freedom to make conscious choices and enjoy liberty to trail to heaven. The beauty of this work is that neither it is sermonizing nor indoctrinating. Allama has drawn his logic on rational points and has skillfully knitted them all together to provide you with an umbrella to protect you in extreme seasons of life. Allama has postulated his theory seeking ground in social anthropology, but his constant dialogue with history, various philosophical schools of thoughts, and other disciplines in social sciences has made it more wholesome, more cosmological seeking unitary knowledge about life and living. Moreover, he has infused the plain text with universal language of love, the classical Sufi poetry, and wisdom of Quran. While translating and editing it, we have tried to consciously pick jargon from other disciplines so that the subject matter and content remains intelligible for many. The telos is to bring harmony and limit the divide. I hope that we are successful. There were certain constraints of time and resources and you may find some language mistakes, or if you feel that we have transgressed Allama's thought or Philosophy, we seek humble forgiveness. I found Allama a very genuine intellectual, honest to his ideas and he has delivered them in cool and calm rationalism. If you find some passionate incursions in the text, attribute it to my ignorance and impulsiveness, as we are still on path, whereas, he has reached his ultimate destination.

I want to offer gracious thanks to Dr. Naderlew for being a great support in finishing this project. I am also greatly indebted to my dean, Professor Khalil Muhammad to empower me with freedom that I may have liberty to use my time my own way. I am also grateful to my ever loving and supporting family, who bear my overindulgence with work with patience and fortitude.

I've re-learned to live wisely; I wish the same for the readers! May Allah help us to move on the right path! Amen!

Seema Arif
Lahore. Pakistan
06-08-2011

About the Book Intelligible Life

Allama was always interested in Human life; he understood it as absolute truth that must be taken seriously. He also believed that "The Nahj-al-Balagheh is a great manifest of the various aspects of a dynamic man on the path to supreme perfection. He regarded the book as original source of knowledge far from "baseless hallucinations or mortal moods of poetic imaginations." However, some people accept to travel on the path of knowledge while others reject and thus distinction is made among believers and non-believers. The 8th volume of his commentary on Nahj-al-Balagheh, which discusses thechoicest values and behaviors that could guide man to the highest ideals in his life, has laid the foundation of this treatise on intelligible life.

He thinks that most of the human beings choose to live in a steel trap of their own uncalculated desires and wishes, simple-mindedly calling it "free life". It is a life molded by "selfish" emotions and actions, busy in breaking rules of nature, thus fighting against God's will, people bring disaster and death to themselves and others. However, Allama would not leave the desperate convoy of humanity to reach its doom. He is quite optimistic in his approach and confidently says:

> "We can state, according to historic documents and man's spiritual qualities, that man can always start from square one again; he can always degrade to zero, and restart his development. He may even get to zero from subzero levels, and then determine his new path... he earnestly prays: Dear God! Will there come a day when these beings who call themselves man and claim to have dominated the universe

come to themselves, for they have not yet done even the
slightest thing to solve their simplest problems?"

Allama would never leave mankind to drown in his "what there is;" he always called man to "what there should be." It would be a sin to leave human life indulged in worldly affairs and some sins are deadly for the development of consciousness in human beings; not only they make the conscience stop functioning, but actually destroy it, creating something "anti-conscience. It is being done by following hedonistic, material and utilitarian approaches in life, which are promoting determinism and fatalism at all levels. He says that "In the confusion of the 20th century, the 21st civilization has put all of mankind up for sale like goods." He said:

"No conscience, no sound mind could be satisfied with
present situation of morality, ethics and virtues; it will ask
itself, 'With all the natural forces and niceties I have, why
shouldn't I use them to serve human beings? Men who have
no advantage over others in love, and no supernatural factor
– God, in fact – to prove their popularity, either. This is the
unsolved mystery Bertrand Russell and I wrote to each other
about and discussed. He, however, had no solution."

Throughout the book he has criticized the material social scientists whose hegemony has arrested the development of humanity as a whole. Naturalism has been the product of desperate attempt of some modern philosophers to align Philosophy with the scientific method of Francis Bacon to pursue knowledge in material world with the five material senses only. Such pursuit has promoted fatalism and determinism of the worst kind, because naturalists tend to see every behavior as biologically determined and adaptive to one's socio-physical environment; human traits and potential is seen as fixed having limited capacity to develop. The pursuit of physical pleasures thus becomes the sole objective in life, as life is temporary and short-lived and it ends here forever. Neither, there is any concept of life-hereafter, nor any realization of divine accountability. Hence, system of meta-values is regarded perennial, unnecessary and must be discarded at the earliest. Personal intelligence is considered enough to code personal morality for oneself. It is not that naturalists completely reject the existence of inner life; they make every attempt to reduce it to the physiology of brain. For them mind is an emergent condition, the function of brain and nothing else. Naturalism defies the existence of supernatural elements like deity, gods or angels and the naturalists negate the existence of a universal mind altogether, not to speak of the capacity of the individual mind to connect with the universal mind.

Therefore, human consciousness is fixated to his life-world-the world of personal perception; a person creates during his her life-time based upon personal experiences with outer reality. It does not merely constitute physical world of objects but social and cultural experiences as well. What is natural means what is common among most of human beings and is included in everyday life experiences; and it constitutes the life-world. It does not include the un-common supra-natural experiences, e.g. mystical experience, and other experiences with high degrees of moral underpinning, such as sacrifice, martyrdom, etc. Allama says:

> "A life empty of prayers and divine attraction is like an empty cup we stick to our lips when we are born, and throw away at death.It is equivalent to death."

> "For any conscious man, each day is like a book full of new lessons. Therefore, we can correctly say that there is a continuous factor called time that can change our ignorance into wisdom... but first, we need those who are really eager for wisdom!"

According to him:

Ideal life means watering and nurturing the ideals of our passing, mortal life from the spring of evolutionary life, finding man and the universe in ourselves, and fulfilling the human character on the path toward eternity. Ideal life is a conscious movement, and passing each stage makes us more eager for the next. The more the eagerness, the greater will be the harmony between the future and the past. This endeavor is led by the human character. A passer of infinity and seeker of eternal perfection by nature, the human character seek the eternal truth, a gust of which has caused waves in the mortal facts of this world. That is ideal life. If a society can give its members a taste of it, it has indeed achieved a truly original civilization.

He is of the view that man is frustrated by the lack of a philosophical system capable of answering all his questions. But we do not need extra ordinary intelligence to embark on this path; only we need to be the seekers of originality – the truth – the idol breakers. There is no need to break away from the tradition either. If somebody is not a hard core modernist and an innovator or is older, even then he/she can take part in reconstruction of knowledge and society.   He defines intelligible life as:

"... a conscious form of life in which the fatalistic forces and activities of natural life are, by means of development, freedom and growth flourished by free will, are adjusted onto the path of relatively evolutionary goals, and the human character is gradually improved in this path until it reaches the supreme aim of life, which is participating in the general harmony of the universe, all of which depends upon divine perfection."

AllamaMuhammad Taghi Jafari was both: the religious-mystic and an open- minded thinker, a combination which is quite rare in Islamic world. In this book we observe a harmony achieved between open mindedness of scientific aptitude,fortitude of religiousness and deep compassion for humanity. He was able to conquer and command the unknown fortresses of "being" and "changing," and with his passion he was able to discover the rule of love that ultimately governs life – the telos of life – the intelligible life.

Allama Jafari believes that once we study the history of human life tells us that people usually choose between two broader styles of life: absolute natural life and intelligible life. Intelligible life style promotes conscious living. Intelligible life style executes personal consciousness in a way that helps individuals to achieve greater self autonomy, control and exercise of free will. Itregulates the deterministic and pseudo-deterministic forces governing natural activities while individuals strive to progress towards higher goals. The scope of intelligible life according to Allama is above and beyond various religious doctrines and ideologies. He prescribes it as the way and means of overcoming the multiple crises Western culture is trapped in, which is enhancing unhappiness, neuroticism and disillusionment among individuals and societies.

Allama Jafari has cautioned that living merely a natural life is akin to animalistic life and those who are immersed into it are struggling for the survival of bodily life preoccupied with satisfaction of their primal instincts and basic needs. Since humanexistencebecomesburdened under the yoke of individuals' carnaldesires, all of its promising and elevating dimensions are neglected by following such a life style. Moreover, travelling down the path of human history, we witness that 'absolute natural life' has left but negative impact upon human will, thought and action. Some of these negative outcomes are as follows:

Thedeparture of constructive love (Ishq) and ambition from our lives, confrontation of right against might, narcissism and self-centeredness, relationships grounded in selfish motives and personal wellbeing, viewing the 'self' as the end and others as the means while understanding that ends would be justifying the means, shattering traditions without anymoral reason, absence of Telos, philosophy and objective of life, nihilism, insecurity and anxiety about the future, self- alienation, inability to reach balanced relationshipbetween self and society,the dissolution of the feeling of "transcendental unity in existence", loosing grip overvarious aspects of one's life by gradual weakening of sublime feelings and humane thoughts, making life-giving foundations of noble cultures unstable, and finally the regrettable failure in interpreting and analyzingconnection between relative and absolute issues.

Allama has identified following principles governing the intelligible life:

1. **Escalated Consciousness:**An individual leading intelligible life chooses to live rationally. The person experiences complete freedom of thought and action and consciously picks values and principles for building up his/her personality and character. Such persons feel complete autonomy in self governing their activities, which are not outcome of any blind following of lives and behaviors of others.

2. **Following the trajectory of elevating goals:**While traveling the path of intelligible life, persons seek excellence both in speech and action; even a singular neural activity is an effort to transform itself into a better one. Intelligible life is seen as progression through certain stages in life; however, it is a continuous journey and at none of these stages of life the wayfarer believes that he/she has reached perfection;therefore seeking continuous improvement in one aspect of life or the other is the job in which seekers are happily engaged throughout their lives.

3. **Charging the free will:** The person who is en route to intelligible life is well aware of the deterministic factors that surround him/her. Taking charge of deterministic and pseudo-deterministic forces of life and making them subjugate to serve one's higher aims and moral purpose of life is the mission of such persons and they enjoy absolute freedom while striving to reach the sublime stage of free will. The more a person utilizes freedom towards free will, the more exalted he/she may feel in realizing the ultimate goal of intelligible life.

4. **Realizing moral purpose of life:**if a person succumbs to the deterministic and pseudo-deterministic desires of the "natural self," then that individual is incapable of reaching the highest goal in life. To reach the most sublime goal in life, one must learn to make intelligent use of mind, which is in harmony with pure conscience and innate perceptions. Finally, one must have a strong will and a serious resolve in order to make sincere efforts to realize the ultimate purpose in life.

5. **Reaching true happiness:**Persons will use internal and external faculties in the most suitable manner on their path to self actualization. As individual's actual potential is realized he/she is able to reach true happiness. During this process raw and elementary sentiments are transformed; they are no more realized as cultural feelings but are sublimated into positive emotions removing negative vibes from life. The persons no more feel themselves dependent on trivial needs of life; instead they develop higher forms of attachments seeking construction in life and society.

Chapter One

The Debacle of Natural Life

This chapter discusses in detail the Western agenda of naturalism and various dilemmas and paradoxes brought into human life as its natural outcomes. Allama Muhammad Taghi Jafari does not completely refute this life style, but regards it as a transient stage of life, which must pass on while continuing on the course of intellectual evolution. The chapter is divided into following sections:

1- Introduction to Natural Life
2- Factors influencing classification of life styles
3- False Claims of Evolution
    a)   *Truth versus Power dilemma!*
    b)   *Male versus Female dilemma!*
    c)   *Dilemma of Futurism*
    d)   *The Dilemma of Imitation*

4- Limitations of Naturalism
5- Pathology of Satisfaction

Introduction to Natural Life

With regards to the division of life styles into: "natural life" and "intelligible life", we start our discussion with natural life.[1]

Everybody knows the fact that human life during its course of evolution has not been a simple and limited phenomenon neither requiring deep thinking nor analysis as it were the living of simple animals. In fact, if we consider human life as a "sudden" phenomenon and not an "emergent" one; it becomes difficult to justify it. The reality of life is a shrouded mystery and while uncovering, we find a number of reasons layered over one another; varying interpretations crowd us when we discuss life's point of origin and development. Some people go for the surface explanation and some go for a little in depth research. For instance, when we read the history of war between two nations by different authors; they provide us with differing opinions though war is a determined phenomenon, but uncovering of the manifold hidden aspects is hard; harder is to find its raison d'être; whether it was merely economical or racism was the sparking plug; what was the role of the avaricious challenges of power between the sovereign rulers in leading to war? As we probe deeper the explanation becomes more difficult as all explanations are coining of human reason having the capacity of generating innumerable possibilities.

> [The task of human reason is perhaps more countering of the false premises to reach pure and the truest one (Kant).]

1-Natural life here signifies living a bodily life in a material world. It is worked out in most worldly fashion, interpreted as akin to animal life, seeking immediate satisfaction of instinctual urges and demands. It does not signify the life of mind, higher purpose or ulterior motives what distinguishes human beings from animals (editor).

On the other hand, there is no doubt that life has not always been taken as a previously established and limited reality in all societies and eras. It has been desirable in every condition for some people, insofar as it is quoted from *Galen*, whohas lamented of the popularity of unexamined life:

I would like to be partially-living [as a man] /Rather than

seeing the world from a mule's anus.[1]

Whether this has rightly been ascribed to *Galen*or not is debatable; similar remarks have been attributed to some other wise men as well. Contrarily, another group of people have such a pessimistic attitude toward life that they say: O'death! Come thou and deliver us from life's swamp. Yet another group of people would assume that they are predestined by natural forces to bear the cumbersome burden of life and they never could have shirked away from this responsibility. For some life is but hedonistic: whenever their life is replete with pleasure they appreciate life as such, and whenever they are deprived of pleasure they are brimming with agony and despair.

Another type of people may move in any direction non-girdled; they are to sail free without having any port of destination to anchor by. They have hardly any concern of what they are doing or what they want. They do not try to understand meaning and purposefulness of life or ever dig deeper to fathom its characteristics and possibilities. Not to mention these, if we pitch in to prepare a statistics of the ideals of contemporary man which constitute his conception of life we could be even more wonder stricken.

A thinker hasnarrated:

"Once I came up with the idea to converse with common

1-Mathnavi'e Ma'navi [Spiritual Couplets of Rumi], book III.

people to know about their most desirable form of life. During the course of these conversations I heard something that was really astounding. For instance, I asked a nurse: what is your favorite form of life? She replied: nursing. I asked again: why? She replied: Since my childhood I've heard from my mother that angels have white wings; therefore, I hold wearing white costumes to be the most desirable ideal of my life. I asked a truck driver: what is your favorite style of life? He replied: truck driving. I enquired: why? His answer was: Since my youth I liked huge things and because of truck's bulkiness I am completely satisfied with driving it, he told with conviction. I asked a well-digger: are you happy with your chosen style of life? He replied: yes, the deeper I dig the well, the more I feel as if I've achieved something high in my life. I took a short break here. It was summer. The well-digger went inside the well and I stood somewhere he couldn't see me and he thought I am gone. I heard him singing a song which says: ...When my eyes hunt for thou O'my swaggering tender gazelle on blooming hills...,

I was amazed what did he saw inside the well so inspiring instead of whirling dew-worms swarming in the stinky and malodorous dark?"

However, ifwe ask our wise friends who have been wriggling along the chain of the history of natural life maintaining a continuous link of investigation about life and its aim and goals, prosperity, enlightenment and virtue, we do not come across into answers which are totally different in spirit as compared to those answers we came across with in aforementioned examples.

Even if we assume that our wise men were but wise and their logic was not contaminated by personal egotism, wadded with conceit in selfish quest of intellectual dominance and prominence, their limited perspectives have done some imperceptible loss to the evolution of human thought, which has been stuck in greedy hunt of material power. Fighting with the mounting pressure of "doing more" if we ask such aggressive hunters of power: what is your criterion of prosperity, virtue, satisfaction and higher purpose of life? Their answer will leave us dumbfounded, not in amazement but in embarrassment, as they would insist: why anyone has to worry about means, our only concern is the "end". I just look for "end" which makes me prosperous, I do not care who serve its means and how? "me" getting satisfied and "my" prosperity makes life all the more meaningful and purposeful and no principle can be more virtuous than the one which gets me such life regardless of its style and the way it is articulated. It is my ultimate goal!![1] No wonder humanity is paying its price dearly with everyday rise in environmental, social and economic problems.

1-Let's try to catch a glimpse of the way one of the patient greedy of power (Mussolini) describes his feelings of satisfaction and prosperity – as we quoted in sixth volume of *Translation and Interpretation of Nahj -ol-Balaghe*:

We reduced the hills to ashes which were thoroughly covered with green jungles. Burning lands and villages, though were misleading, amused us!!

As you see by yourself, how much pleasure have brought this greedy of power the burning lands, animals and men.... Insofar as he says:

O' my God! I remember how hastily the animals were to flee... you know! It was amazing, when I could blow the chaffy roof of a local house which was wholly camouflaged with huge trees!

Let's pay a close attention! This crazy greedy of power doesn't say: I killed my dangerous enemy to save my life, but he says: "you know! It was amazing" what was amazing? Burning the chaffy roof of local houses inside which were live people! Next phrase shows the ultimate meaning of pleasure, prosperity, satisfaction and life-goal for this greedy of power who says:

After being the spectators of my heroic enterprise, the residents of hut escaped... five thousands Ethiopians, who were surrounded within the fire, unwillingly were pushed to the end of fire line, where a fiery hell was settled. [*Power*, Bertrand Russell]

Pioneers of the convoy of humanity and some celebrated personalities, such as holy prophets and other people with mature minds and liberated consciousness had quoted only one purpose of life: to invite human beings to "Intelligible Life". They have all tried to introduce the people to the vicissitude of natural life and the truth of "Intelligible Life", with the hope to reduce the number of people who will choose to live natural life, and thus more will join the caravan of "Intelligible Life".

Generally speaking:

From the very beginning of the history of mankind, there have been various reasons which make it mandatory that a fresh outlook must be provided to common people about their understanding of life as they generally live it; moreover, people who want to experience self-actualization want guidance in order to improve their practices as well as understanding of life.

Every revealed religion which has been preached by a holy prophet strongly insists that: never should we enslave "*Hayāt* [**Leben**]" to our natural desires which, causes its development to slow down. Life has been traveling through its purely natural course and this majestic phenomenon has finally arrived at the excellent stage of sensing "autonomy" and realization of power of self-development and improvement, therefore, we should not barricade its development by dictating: this is the last destination. Not only did not they dismiss any natural fact in human life, revealed religions have always ordered human beings to flourish all their nature-given aptitudes, but commanding so they have never shut their eyes on the subject of human natural and physical pleasures.

They have merely recommended us to establish a harmony between these natural desires and nature-given aptitudes – may it help us to be benefited much more. All religious rules have been established to guarantee the unceasing development of life:

Let's have a sharp eye on us moving while being seatedDon't you see we are the harbingers of a new land?[1]

Religious rules lead the man through an eternal track:

From the sea we came and so we will return to the seaFrom the heaven we came and so we will return to the heaven.[2]

By observing the consequences of being plunged into "natural life", we would never come across anything special but mundane pleasures, getting some-things from "the nature" and then returning back the same. For instance, farmers harvest their crops after much toil, but reaping once is never enough, they have to continue with the cycle of plowing, sowing, growing and reaping again and again. Recognizing oneself as merely a natural product of copulation, the reality of man is reduced to nothing but that of a marionette that is manipulated with the whirlwinds of natural laws, as **Saebe Tabrizi** says:

Everyone who came to this grievous world like a whirlwindHad sands for a while, and finally did he wind inward and left.

Or as another poet says:

Like a pen we pass through the tablet of existenceHaving authored the story of our grieves we passThrough this stormy sea which paces toward its endContinuously we pass like the waves following each other.

The most grievous outcome is highlighted, more pernicious than above-mentioned effect, what is permanent? It is only the "struggle for existence" – the ultimate gift for mankind by

---

1-Mathnavi'e Ma'navi [Spiritual Couplets of Rumi], book VI.
2-Divan-e-shams-e-Tabrizi (Love Poems of Rumi).

nature for living purely a natural life. Still, the majority of human societies are stuck in living such life, unable to break away with the trail of natural history of animal life and enter *anthropo-historia*or begin with the experienceof human life. It is not merely by accident that throughout the pages of human history we hardly find any page in which some lines are not written in cold blood. Even the lines telling the story of uneventful ordinary life have all been contaminated with a sense of loss of freedom and happiness where words like "deterministic" and "what should be done" express human sense of loss and failure. The sages, therefore duplicate the ideas already presented by the holy prophets, that life "must" have a justified purpose – not only explaining "why" to live but also highlighting "how" to live.

There are many genuine concerns of humanity, which have found diverse expressions in different societies and cultures, as they celebrate the existence of "common sense", "primordial nature", "consciousness", "conscience" and "heart" etc. The subtle aspects of human nature command the necessity of transforming the pure natural life to noble life [*Viva Intelligibilis*] through which human unseen potential is flourished granting the super-unity of human life.

The ethnographic studies of human history and civilization increase despondence and dismay in what we call "human" so to say, therefore why to conduct such studies or the studies which reduce human experience to the primal unilateral status of animal life? The prior would bitterly fail in explaining hard core intricacies of human nature and the later would be turning a blind eye to all noble deeds and productive human attitudes in history because our history is rich of living examples of people whose life could be explained as extensions of "Intelligible Life" or at least as semi-intelligible.

The convoy of holy prophets, saints and developed minds has always been moving shoulder to shoulder with large numbers of those ordinary people who have but resigned to living an absolute natural life. Despite of some pessimistic allusions, developed minds in "Intelligible Life" have not been just a bunch of exceptions. Moreover, their nature did not exist in complete opposite of those who love to lead a simple natural life. Contrarily, one should admit that people submerged in natural life have unknowingly missed the natural course of humanity by nullifying their reason, conscience and other humane attitudes. Unfortunately, they were led to the wrong track by listening to the call of their bodies and physical world around them, while they completely missed the opportunity to uncover their latent potentials and hidden capacity to approach the "Intelligible Life". The hidden treasures are for travelers who dare to enter no-man's land with respect with an aim to share or to conserve what is pure and thus precious and not for the merchants and mercenaries, who have insatiable greed to hold, possess and command the course of life.

Factors influencing classification of life styles

Human beings may choose to live life on totally different planes: "Natural Life" and "Intelligible Life" due to following reasons.

1) **Internal factor or personal reasons**: the reasons underlying this factor are grounded in natural human instincts[1] which

---

1-Instincts: All creatures are born with specific innate knowledge about how to survive; such knowledge is called instinct. Instincts are generally understood as innate complex behaviors that are rigidly patterned throughout a species and it is hard to unlearn them. Such behaviors are governed by autonomic nervous operate autonomously without being subjected to any external societal law.

However, natural instincts help us only in physical survival by satisfying our basic needs, such as hunger, sleep and sex. These instincts or drives have a strong element of desire added to them. Moreover, instincts create urgency in human body demanding for quick gratification. It becomes hard to deal with the bubbly excitement and effervescence caused by instincts and fulfilling desires seems most exciting solution as they relieve human body of the tension and pain caused by it. However, complying behaviors may or may not be conforming to moral norms; thus meeting desires can pose serious challenges, which can only be overcome by developing self esteem and taking one's reason and conscience seriously.

2) **External factor or social reasons**: the reasons underlying this factor are grounded in relationships, the necessity of which stems from gregariousness, the need to live in a group or community.

Despite the fact that human beings are endowed with innumerable potencies and privileges over other creations, challenges related to gaining order and balance in social life are not adequately met. The enormous feat of acquiring 'style of life' corresponding to dominating cultures has cost people heavily resulting in loss of some of prominent individual human dispositions. These two factors have led the people to be divided into two main groups:

a) People belonging to the first group find it very hard to manage the impulsiveness of their natural instincts, thus their attention remain focused upon gratification of basic

---

system and do not require any regulation of rational mind or consciousness to perform (editor).

needs. Taking care of these needs, they have devoted themselves to such life purviews which have been contrived for peaceful coexistencewhile living in any society. They do not challenge existing norms or prevailing laws related to satisfaction of needs in their respective societies. These are the very people who form the convoy of "naturalism"[1] and unfortunately they have always been in the majority in human societies throughout history.

b) People who have always taken sound moral reasoning as leading principles of their life and seek constant guidance from their conscience to examine the existing norms and laws of social living. By taking this stance they have committed themselves for development of their mental and spiritual potential on the one hand and moral behavior of the society on the other.

Moreover, these developed minds have never enslaved themselves to the style of life which is enforced by any society or culture upon them; rather they have always accepted those social norms which they found inescapable. While they strive to adjust to the prevailing life style of a society, they also seek ways for improvement by exercising personal social influence. Even being in minority, these people form the convoy of "The Intelligible Life" having more spiritual tranquility within themselves while exhibiting a strong sense for understanding the life process as a whole.

While seeking reasons to understand why so many people are inclined to join the convoy of "Naturalism" instead of entering "Intelligible Life", we need to find out the basic differences among these two groups of people, because

---

1-See Part A for further explanation.

apparently neither they differ in their physiology – biological make-up or mental make-up. Both groups are humans as Aristotle, Caligula and Nero share the same definition for being a human. This shared definition which merely represents "human primitive nature as it is" has resulted in neglecting "human nature as it ought to be"; rather it has even been deployed as a disguised moral to promote "human primitive nature as it is"

Human nature is by default gregarious, it demands to live amid other people in accordance with society. However, even after admitting this absolute necessity of social life, people never forgo the idea that their individual dispositions are unique contributions to the aggregate – society. With this analysis we come to an important conclusion: social life itself and the relative disciplines dictating its norms dictate the future of human beings prescribing a particular style to it, either "Naturalism" or "The Intelligible Life". It is evident, however, from history that authorities defining norms and laws for social life are always bent towards naturalisminstead of intellectualism. Every effort has been carried out at large for actualizing the very ideals of social life, rather than preparing human beings to enter in "The Intelligible Life" which, in fact develops human conscience, rationality and frees human consciousness from unnecessary doubts and skepticism.

Thinkers like **EmileDurkheim,** while recognizingsociety as the basic reality have been unable to realize the complex and intricate knots that have tied the relationship between the individual and the society. Their views are biased and cover partial reality only, and tend to violate the basic balance that exists in human nature, never realizing that they are escalating extremism of another kind, causing superficial trivialities to supersede real issues people are confronted with. Thus, public attention is drawn away from the root cause of problems as they are stuck in defining nature of the problem. Such thinkers must be well aware more than anyone else that social life, with its predestined mechanisms, has nothing to do with the obligations and values that help people to pave their way to success in securing an intelligible interpretation of their individual lives.

The cry for "equality and fraternity", which has been clearly resonant in all societies during recent centuries, refrains from being associated with its necessary addendum: "mankind should incessantly seek for a free and virtuous conscience", for fealty that it may be blamed for being moralistic. Before going into the details of the tragic consequences of such extremist beliefs in naturalism, I'd like to point out two important outcomes here: on one hand, people become skeptical about ordinary people's ability to manage their natural instincts and on the otherthey hesitate and lag in developing reason andmoral conscience. The study of these consequences will be our second premise. However, I'd like to point out here clearly that having taken these consequences into consideration, the claim of continuous rational evolution of humanity needs a comprehensive revision.

False Claims of Evolution

Deep study of human history unfolds myriad of problems and issues that one is flabbergasted to acknowledge how we have survived so many issues and problems? The same is true for the claims of natural evolution of life and the projected intellectual [Intelligible] one. It remains debatable whether the claim for "Intellectual Evolution" is admissible or we should consider it merely a consoling slogan for dressing the wounds of those perfection seeking minds who have been suffering throughout history by seeing their wishes for development bubble into air with the hot winds of pessimism blowing strongly around them.

I have no doubt at all about the intended goodness of great human initiatives, especially about those which are recently been taken for distinguished technological, scientific and industrial developments. My brows are raised with concern on seeking much pending answer of very important questions: whether we have reached the desired outcomes for humanity at large? Whether the achievements suit the invaluable capabilities, talents and privileges with which human beings are endowed with. We have taken centuries to become familiarized with the human talent; thus, we reserve the right of expressing our deep down concern about evolution and know whether this evolution is really an intelligent one, moving on its right course towards human rational development "The Intelligible Life" or it has lost its way on the path of lowly naturalism.

If we are to give an answer, which is substantiated by purely objective evidences, without referring to any ethnic epic poetry or other self-addressed compliments, while answering, the Pandora Box of all issues and complaints must be opened and we need to examine in detail the problems which we the human beings have been struggling with for many centuries while taking due course of natural life. We should not discuss this issue through those syllogisms which are totally founded on Aristotelian a priori principles and abstractions of our personal inferences, since we may reach the same reality by taking a quick scan of the written and unwritten confessions of contemporary thinkers.[1]

1-Such books as: "Civilized Man's Eight Deadly Sins" by **Konrad Lorenz,** "Armored World, Starved World" by **Willy Brant,** "Man, The Unknown Being" **Alexis Carrel** and "The Philosophy of Nihilism" by **Albert Camus.**

Before even starting my discussion about the current issues faced by naturalists, I would like to acknowledge and make it clear that I do not intend to underscore the utility of taking naturalistic course of life or to reject this style of life altogether as it will lead to extremism of another kind resulting in nothing else but the denial of human rationality, belief in free will and right of choice. Moreover, by doing so, I do not intend to overlook the standpoint taken by all those believers of Ishq, conscientiousness, constructive initiatives and perfectionism. It will be cutting my own wings since human dynamism has the power to delimit skies parting distances between earth and heaven to ascend to the threshold of ultimate Truth. Yes, I cannot dismiss the power of Love, which may have its seed in physics of "Natural Life", assigning individuals a variety of aptitudes and privileges.

To state the matter differently, however, I reiterate that we reserve the right to explore logic that states ways and behaviors differentiating between our expectancy "human being as it ought to be" and "human being as it is" – the actual product or outcome. The challenge here lies in the question, whether wonderful scientific achievements could mask all the agony humanity has gone through by choosing to live a hedonic life subservient to immediate and short-lived pleasures living merely a physical life entails. The harder question is whether these human achievements (scientific so to say) are the outcome of living naturally or intellectually? If the answer is in the favor of the latter, then why we are spending invaluable resources to indulge people in hedonistic pleasures rather than calling people to live a simple but intelligent and purposeful life?

Human beings are not lifeless; they are neither devoid of movement nor of volition – capacity to choose direction in which way to move. Therefore, while taking care of this argument about the choice of human beings about their lifestyle (natural or intellectual), I am not talking of stones or sand. We may expect from stones that they may be pushed into any direction or can be crafted into desired shape because they are not "intelligent"; so stones can be expected to stay the same "the stone as it is" and we would never ever comment that: "the stone should be intelligent, conscientious and they must have some Ishq - constructive love" yearning for some goal and travelling to reach a destination in life. But we may expect from any human being [The Individual Person] to be "the man as it is in whom lies great potential for becoming, multilevel advancement, thus reaching natural expectations "the man as it ought to be [The Ideal human being]". The gap between these two poles of continuum seems huge and difficult to part as it explains what is expected from human beings and what their actual performance is.

If we narrow down this expectancy, the balance is tilted downwards, limiting human capacity to its biological potential of what human race has discerned through course of its natural history. The sad news gives us a shock that majority of people will continue their life on physical plane - living for existence but dying in nothingness. Of course, few exceptions would be there, the sedulous convoy of the minority who could transform their meager physical life into the intelligible one.

Next we deal with those problems which human race is struggling with during the pursuit of natural life.[1]

> *I tell you the bitter storyMay I thus to purify you of all bitterness.*[2]

1-If **Rumi** was to discuss about these problems, he would start with the verse quoted above.

I am also hinting toward the same principle, if you expose your pains thoroughly, they will find their treatment too.

2-Mathnavi'e Ma'navi [Spiritual Couplets of Rumi], book III.

Pure natural sciences or for that matter social sciences, none of them disregards the value of human consciousness. Taking the example of an anthropologist, for instance or a mathematician, wouldn't he acknowledge that human consciousness as one of the most genuine and loftiest of products ever created or existed? Hardly anyone would be denying the fact; rather our worthy opponents would offer a carefree reply: Does this need any debate? Isn't it a common sense? We don't need any intellectual effort or individual experiences to fathom the fact: "whoever is more conscious is more alive [human]". However, we witness the end of this quest for naturalism with Maulana Rumi:

> *From their liberty and existence/ all world escape to their inebriated headfor a moment of emancipation from their consciousnessthey putthemselvesto shame with intoxication and narcotizationthey all have supposed the existence to be nauseatingAnd free will appears to them all as purgatory.*[1]

According to Rumi, under temporary tranquilizing effects resulting from inflated ego, people tend to flatter themselves with the idea that: universal laws of nature, are not integrated in themselves unless one uses them rationally and consciously,as ifhuman consciousness could dominate divine consciousness; as if these laws were the chains they were entangled with and freedom lies in liberation from these laws. They ignore the fact that the man who has already been shackled by the chain of these laws never could tear it by biting:

1-Mathnavi'e Ma'navi [Spiritual Couplets of Rumi], book VI.

O' hunted prey! You bite the ropeNo biting would tear this rope.[1]

They forget that unwinding of rope and disentanglement of chains is breaking down of links through which one could ascend to the realm of "Intelligible Life". The sesame is not 'conscious' but the conscientiousness; and the solution is not breaking the chain but holding it like a rein. Breaking invites destruction and so we are witnessing all around us. Contemporary human cultures have been viciously cleared out of Ishq- constructive love from which all goods and perfections originate. No matter our reasons are enslaved by worthless whim wham. If we were able to trace the continuity of human will and actions which enabled the humans to take all those great steps which they have taken in relation to the world and other human beings back to their primary incentives, we would see nothing but true love:

Love is the whole [word], and we are the letters,it is the Red Sea and we are the dropletsGiving us hundreds of reasons and we have resisted each single one.[2]

In love, you shall find other intelligible More glorious and precious than these intelligible.[3]

Human Love is the primary cause of its being and becoming. The understanding of surviving and thriving of the whole human race can be culminated into a single word – love – small yet the most powerful.

1-Divan-e-shams-e-Tabrizi.

2-Divan-e-shams-e-Tabrizi.

3-Mathnavi'e Ma'navi [Spiritual Couplets of Rumi], book V.

In the history of human intelligible life, there is not a single great initiative, whether material or spiritual, impregnated by "liberty" and "will", which has not been motivated by true love. On the other hand in doctrine of naturalism "love" only appears as a psychic representation which has its root in human sexual instinct which homo-sapiens have in common with other animals. This instinct might be even more pleasurable for other animals than poor homo-sapiens because animals do not bear any cost for this pleasure. I would choose to describe this natural feeling differently; the human attachments have found other loci of attention; such feelings may now be displaced for desire of material objectives. The intoxication could be worst on conscious/unconscious exposure to strong appeal of important positions, high ranks, wealth and popped up showbiz fame. It is not unwise to admit that even this mundane sexual appeal between the two genders has not disclosed its true meaning yet - the meaning as was expressed once:

> In love nights, where life's sapling is implanted,Luminous torch of life passes from hand to hand at the gate of eternity.[1]

It is easy to recognize the relationship between genders as a natural phenomenon with all possible explanation of human sexual instinct in purely biological terms rather than understanding the lofty incentives and pleasures which have their root in a divine conception of creation. Anyone may object what is so sacred and divine about human sexual relationships as it has been celebrated in primitive cultures – if the element of divine conception of life makes it sacred then what is so lowly and baser about it – the characteristic being shared with animals....? Why not my ears sound the voice: All bodily

---

1-First part of the sentence is byGoethe, and the rest has been added by *Allama Jafari* himself.

pleasures will end with body, but all loftier thoughts, all feelings and emotions of care, all attitudes of concern and behaviors of sharing and sacrifice exhibited in human relationships will transcend with us up and above this earthly plane of existence.

Truth versus Power dilemma!

"Whether truth is triumphant or power?" Knowing that the truth is purely mental abstraction and the power is a physical phenomenon, the latter question, would be rather an indelibly disgraceful confession to our hearts that the professed journey wayfarers of the natural history took on the way of evolution towards civilization has never been really taken and we are back at square one drawing our unconscious and brute animal selves to surface again. It is restoring our journey backwards and experiencing all that tension, negative emotion vibes that human beings face in any emergency situation when survival is threatened. The choice lies with us whether will we deny the question altogether, resort to some rationalization or we will muster some courage to face the truth.

Isn't power the most fundamental source of movement and change in both realms of humanity and natural world? Power and force are definitely the most fundamental source of *becoming* in the world. Having turned a blind eye on the *Platonic* radical idea quoted by **Whitehead** "Being is Potentiality"; we call attention to a popular saying frequently cited in all authoritative Islamic sources:

There is no power but that which has already been caused by divine power.[1]

Now, we must pitch in to understand why the evolutionary thinkers have set "Truth versus Power dilemma", instead of attributing power and truth to the same source. Having set this dilemma, they also dare to confess that: power lacks truth, power corrupts truth or at least, power in human possession loses its truth! Analyzing such comments, should we infer here that human beings are failure, who have not actually achieved any success in logically settling their issues like that of power vs. truth. Shall we further admit that humans are weaklings inherently faulty by design - a failure product or creation? Such comments have the capacity to blur the brightness of "Truth" at one hand, but on the other it may bring spurious peace to those souls who have experienced a painful defeat of power.

Centuries have passed and human sciences are still in infancy to describe human phenomenon. Whether are they philosophers, psychologists or other people from humanitarian disciplines, they keep coining different philosophies and theories about supremacy of human cognition over bodily forces, but theories are missing in action. One wonders where things go wrong: Serious natural disaster occurs when Psychology seeks to explain human behavior through seeking explanation from purely physical sciences like Biology giving rise to more and more deterministic and fatalistic attitudes and pushing people in gory pit of darkness and disappointment. Isn't it another disgrace added to dethrone human beings from eternally granted divine position?

Psychologists have blatantly tried to apply principles of heredity - inherited experiences and investigations of past.

1-See for instance: Holy Quran, Nahjol-Balaghah and Sahife Sajadieh.

Despite all these efforts, however, it is still difficult to define human identity which will distinguish its individual position as "existing being". What is "ego" and what is "self"? Do these two concepts completely encompass the identity of human being it totality as stated above? Still people are waiting to get a comprehensive explanation of their causal being "Self or Ego", to which one may reduce all grief and pains. May we open our eyes one fine morning, during our life-time, to call it our day – the day of deliverance -"true dawn of happiness" when there will be no mind-body division.

Though it has already been made clear to people that "Egotism"[1] is the psychic illness which ruins "human true self", however, no remedy has yet been found by scientists and clinicians for this fatal illness. The interesting question here is: do they render it an illness? Though much energy and talent has been spent to describe "self" and "ego" by our worthy psychologists and other social scientists, yet little or no effort has been spent on investigation of socially mal-adaptive egos, causing social and ethical problems rather than clinical ones. Even if somebody found a resuscitative cure prescribed by religion and ethics, he/she may not have the necessary talent to use it or do not express enough faith to practice it.

Alas! With much regret and disappointment felt on valued time and effort being wasted, I profess: if celebrated men of science would have used only a few of opportunities and mental energies, that were missed due to certain egotistic

---

1-Egotism is defined by Webster's dictionary as the tendency to speak or write of oneself excessively and boastfully. It is understood in terms of inflated ego attaching too much importance to oneself, attributes as self conceit. Egotism is defined here by psychologists Roy Baumeister and Liqing Zhang as "the motivation to maintain and enhance favorable views of one's self." In Sufism it is regarded as spiritual sickness which when uncontrolled may lead to denial of the existence of God or proclaiming equivalence with Prophets or God (editor).

attitudes while walking through natural course of modern science in recent past for this long lost personal-social development issue, where would we may have reached now in our destination towards prescribed evolution - civilized and peaceful humanity.

In religion each measure taken to oppose natural laws is perceived as evil. But in egotist state of mind, it is not unnatural to be biased and judgmental against people having opposing views, so why they should care for ethics and values; these are after all our self-coined terms. Experiencing nature as tough, challenging and hard to conquer has led to the oppressive and coercive views of nature and thus God. In their temporary moments of triumph, sometimes people of natural science completely want to relish individual victory, however small it may be, while completely banishing from their consciousness the holistic order of universe. Narrow-mindedness breeds extremism. This statement is true and much valid for people having scientific mindset and research aptitudes than any other, because they forget to acknowledge that their achievement how grand it may be is just a mole hill, keeping in view the discipline, subject area, topics and width and breadth of their findings in context of grand design of life as whole.

Even more disappointing than this loss is the fact that: instead of trying to turn his steps toward the path of perfection and goodness, man is such an impertinent fool that his persistent blind wish for rapid progress in the physical course of life has made the world a great scene for evil, so that we could say: it would not be surprising if you read or heard someday that someone has stricken back a slap with a shot! Rather you will be surprised when a punch is revoked by forgiveness and mercy, and not with revenge and rudeness!

When use of physical power is seen as the only solution and not the moral power, the whole world of perception and action is deteriorated. For instance, an envoy of the state comes to his particular mission area and encountering some morally immoderate people there, he warns them strictly: if you are bully, then I am the Bull itself. Unfortunately, the history of human natural life has always been so that some indignant people light up the fire of evil and corruption, and the others only try to be the bull, not the human, without making any effort to kill the evil fire. As if finite evil and corruption is nothing but an excuse to pave the way for infinite waves of evil and corruption!

Unfortunately, people tend to take extreme positions when our judgments of others' personalities are confronted with opposing views or conflicting perspectives, coloring our smart principles and values grey. Narrow-mindedness of the most of men of science which has its root in their blind enthusiasm for the subject-matter they have taught or researched leaves terrible effects on social environment as well as knowledge culture.

It is but due to the fact that human vision has limited scope and there are too many chances of getting illusioned. As Master Rumi commands: in order to activate real vision, we may have to shut our physical eye. This statement is not limited to closing of eyes and get lost in self activated delusions or fantasy with sense of glory attached with selfish pursuits – Egotism. Rather vision requires activating mechanism attached with internal perception – ego – to connect with Divine intellect and try to perceive and understand natural laws – the Divine Order of Universe. It is divine because no human/another being have been able to change or alter it so far. Confronted with this truth, men of natural science have perceived it in stark opposition, taking 'nature' as enemy posing threats to physical survival of human beings and their creations, which always remain ordinary, temporary and perishable as the human beings themselves are. Therefore, science and religion seem to face each other dagger drawn at opposite poles and we witness the world at war.

However, grandiose concepts attached with "power of science" on the superstructure of physical aspects of human life have made scientific pursuit very charming for people. This charm makes them crazy votary of 'power ascribed to scientific ideas' wildly beseeching and trying to grapple any aspect of physical life; thus deteriorating worthy human beings into a living example of what is known as:"*Homo homoni lupus*[1] [Man is a wolf to [his fellow men]" or Man is such a being whose essence is totally contingent upon *Libido*[2][Sexual Instinct]". We have hardly any other better alternatives or explanations available from our esteemed community of enlightened scholars. The bitterness is not limited to such explanations only. Further pain is added when scholars do not agree in their viewpoints and keep differing from each other adding to confusion of people.

The accounts of human history popular these days is fraught with accounts of describing human relationships as an outcome of human nature as described above – a deceptive wolf or crazy sexual maniac. Thus the conceived image of human being projects nothing in itself but that of animalism and brutality. To get relieved of this psychological pain, people altogether dismiss the idea of getting to the truth of their "being". It is not the scene itself but sometimes the eyes that experience the scene matter the most because they will describe it according to their personal experience, shaped itself by background knowledge or

---

1-First attested in *Plautus' Asinaria*("lupus est homo homini"), the sentence was drawn on by Thomas Hobbes in the dedication of his work *De cive* (1651) (translator).

2-Freud believes that libido is our life force, driving us not only to the sexual activities but to the refrigerator, the mall, yoga, and a painting class (translator).

personal aptitude. What matters most to us today are our material needs and day to day wants, which keep our attention clouded for most of the time and the same is highlighted in our interpretation of history – our selfish interests and wants, our jealousies and our fights.

Themost vicious exploitation of the "mean-ends" relationship, that is, to prescribe commission of any act to achieve any goal which appears to be desirable for the powerful and ignoring the maxim that: that goal is allowed to make a mean its victim that has an equal value with it, or even is more valuable, so it can thwart any possible loss. It leads to extremism and autocratic thoughts as propounded by Machiavellian Philosophy that "means may not justify the ends" corrupting the morals of a society and thus hampering the natural course of a developing civilization. I wonder that such bargaining is allowed in societies, who profess to enlighten human thought and action by revival of old Greek rationalism. How could they refute Aristotle's principle of "Golden Mean" by renting out their souls to Sophism?

These naturalist historians while advocating their viewpoints not only contend themselves with bloodshed, injustice and corruption done by people but they recognize their "errors" as human tragedy and rejoice by fitting people like Nero and Caligula into character of a hero and masking personal weaknesses in the weakness of their heroes. Thus, in order to justify all that is wrongly done, philosophies are fabricated to orchestrate the brutish *weltanschauung* the leitmotif of which is: "*world is the place of struggle for existence between the strong and the weak*" – adding insult to injury, the powerful must cull the weak rather than protecting them.

[Just take the case of Africa,] how many beautiful natural landscapes and life-giving space of the earth has been destroyed, changing it into willful battlegrounds, weaponry companies taking in charge, and preparing the scene for the parade of evil antihuman forces. Not only invaluable mental and material resources have been vandalized in this largest continent, the professed birthplace of homo-sapiens according to evolutionary science. Who have committed these unpardonable sins – the genocide of the natural residents and homicide of the surviving ones, threatening the diversity and of dynamism of life itself?

Alas! We are still to reach a vision for the universal ideal to see ourselves as master creation – the *Insa'n* – the object of attention, great ideal in itself and the final station that leads to ultimate destination where means and ends converge in itself to proclaim: All is One.

Male versus Female dilemma!

Unfortunately, both the genders have constantly being provoked sexually in the name of "perennial love", though still confusion lurks when we contend the divide between two genders whether it is a natural divide or the contrived one we keep arguing about. Is it physical or psychological? If the "love" is perennial – an old fashioned habit, then one should forget about it as other forms of bodily pleasures are available, such as gay or lesbian life style. Such thoughts are prevalent in modern society, putting at risk the most natural of human relationships at stake, as the risk runs to destroy all important relationships related to family and not just the small unit – husband and wife?

Someofpsychologists have proclaimed their disappointment of the possibility of a logical harmony between man and woman:

> *The possibility of a perfect logical harmony between man and woman, as a couple, is to the same degree that to cut an apple*

in two and throw each one to a corner of a jungle of vast
extent. Then to wish a wind to come and reunify them!![1]

Such confusions in understanding role of genders have been
continued without being aware of how much pernicious it has
been, instead of being constructive. We are in urgent need of
answering the question whether the relationship between two
genders can be "naturalized" in modern society or it will be
accepted as just another standardized but conventional
connection, highly orthodox and limiting human freedom?

Moreover, the impossibility of discerning any transcendental
unity in vital and mental [intellectual] respects of human life
has resulted in "unauthentic and colorless personalities" in the
course of human self-development. All of these concerns leave
us no choice but to lament over the inefficiency of our
intellectual community of social scientists, philosophers to
speak more of harmony of mind and body as an integrated
whole and do not study human physical and mental
[intellectual] life in compartments.

For example, we could mention extensive researches about
sexual instinct, theories describing logical construction of
thought mechanisms, unremitting efforts for describing and
interpreting human will, and considerable over-precisions
about: intelligence, association of ideas, imagination, legal
issues, economic condition, political interactions, artistic
activities and many others are performed in isolation.
Hundreds of other phenomena which are regarded as
peculiarities of human mental life have been demarcated in a
way as if they have nothing in common with each other;
unaware of the fact that human mental life, besides these

1-See: *A Commentary of Nahj Al-Balaghe*, M.T. Jafari vol. 11/The Harmony
between Man and Woman.And See: www.ostad-jafari.com, Selections of
writing, Menandwomen: A serious study.

contractual empirical units, has a transcendental unity only through which it could tread on the course of evolutionary development, and not with disintegrated units which as soon as they are broken apart they miss the mental life.[1]

Here we are sensing gradual induction of independent human personalities into unauthentic and colorless lifestyles, which in any color will surely be under the spell of unconscious determinism – occasionally being painted red under spell of sexuality or black under magic of free will.   Furthermore, de-emotionalizing of human has gradually deteriorated "persons" into lifeless objects or "things"- another blunder of careless reductionism. This reduction in turn results in the disappearance of self-independence and thus surrendering to the stronger factors, without being able to make any effort to acquire power for retrieving its independence. The ruining outcome of this process is the disappearance of "autonomy" which is the most significant distinguishing feature of living beings as compared to inanimate nature. Exercise of will is contingent upon human emotions. When handcuffed and separated from reason emotions are left with no choice but to surrender before brute power of physical-social needs of life. One has to admit: Yes! This is reality; autonomy, self respect and esteem, all bubble away leaving cold bland water to be taken sip by sip instead of an invigorating fizzy drink.

Dilemma of Futurism

While examining the theory of evolution, *Konrad Lorenz* has identified several operational mismanagements in designing

---

1- Such a disintegrated knowledge is like catching a fish and then to cut it into pieces and when it is in frying-pan on fire we pitch in to know its peculiarities. That is another way of conceptualizing the compartmentalization of knowledge in modernist episteme.

live and sustainable organic systems by human beings, which he has described in detail in his seminal work, *Civilized Man's Eight Deadly Sins*.[1] Some of these have caused serious maladies in societies arresting their development and initiating their decay. I strongly condemn such behaviors, especially unwarranted violations of the tradition, not only it has weakened the pillars of genuine cultures which are all established upon "dynamism" and "Telesis (purposefulness)", missing the goal and philosophy of life has led to increased tendency toward nihilism in its different forms. Such fatalism can be defeated only by developing alternative perspectives on life promoting faith and hope in life and the living. Therefore,

---

1-**Konrad Zacharias Lorenz** (Vienna, 7 November 1903 – Vienna, 27 February 1989) was an Austrian zoologist, naturalist, ornithologist and Nobel Prize Laureate (translator). According to him sin is described as a conscious offence of rules; it has a prominent position in Christian axiomatic, which has contributed substantially for designing principles for cultural specific morality in Christian societies. The etiologist Konrad Lorenz has enlisted eight mortal sins, which he considers conscious mistakes of the rational mind and sophisticated cultures. Unless corrected, these sins will disrupt human societies resulting in effacing of humanity on earth. The sins are:

a) Overpopulation,

b) Devastation of environment,

c) Economical competition between people,

d) Emotional burnout – human fixation to desire and rejection of suffer,

e) Genetic decay - possible origin of regressive social behavior, only few selective factors except of natural feeling for justice and some traditional ideas of what is right and wrong, keep the norms of social behavior upright , infantile hedonism.

f) Break up with tradition – underestimation of irrational cultural foundation of our knowledge, superior rationality, and escalated conflict between generations,

g) Growing pliability to doctrines – diseases of science are culturally caused after Lorenz, fashion advertisement have negative impact, the most destructive in the world of science,

h) Nuclear weapons – the least dangerous sin, threat of nuclear destruction as catalyst of irresponsibility to future.

thinkers who promote skepticism over worldviews and disillusionment must be countered seriously, such as the one who says: ["Angst is the disorder of twentieth century".][1] Such despair is introjected into others because of thinkers' personal inability of explaining their own *weltanschauung*. If thinkers were able to explicitly propound their conception of "worldview", they would never make people depressed under the paradoxical plethora of their *weltanschauung*.

Futurism is a consequence of turning a blind eye to today and yesterday and thus tearing down the reality in disjointed pieces of time. On examining the history of "Naturalism", any one may remark that for hundreds and thousands of years now humanity is trying to sustain abjectly in projected illusions of "tomorrow" in a semi-conscious state of mind, whereas, the true human self remains buried under veils of "Naturalism". Consequently, people never ever miss the presence of yesterday and today in their lives, and thus they never seeks liberation from imaginary tomorrows planted in their consciousness. Yet there are people who tend to seek refuge in today or yesterday rather than caring for tomorrow, while others have crafted the image of an ideal tomorrow deep inside themselves when their dreams will come true.

As a poet says:

> *My life fell a victim to my tomorrowAlas from this blind tomorrow of mine.*[2]

1-This concept has frequently been used by many Existentialists to describe man's situation in the modern world. (editor)

2-This verse is of Nadher Zadeh Kermani.

This personally crafted life-world[1]has resulted in malady of "self-alienation".[2]

Furthermore, failing to realize the promised good of democracy, the incumbent authorities keep their promises at bay that were given to people during election campaigns on one hand and on the other indeterminacy of the real dominion of authorities in societies – balancing of rights and responsibilities among working institutions of the society, initiating an internal competition for power and corrupting discipline and social order of the society. **Alfred North Whitehead**, indeed, has attributed this indeterminacy to the intricacy of human nature itself:

> *Human nature is so complex that plans for society are to statesmen not worth even the price of the defect paper.*[3]

Deplorable inability to distinguish between the relatives and the absolutes is not merely a philosophical issue insignificant enough to overshadow life and its desirable peculiarities, but it is such an issue which must be tackled conscientiously; otherwise both the individual and the society would not be able to design and manage their mental and social lives or even justify their material and spiritual states.

Modern Art is also promoting waywardness in the name of non-conventionalism. By reducing it to mere nudity and

---

1- See Part A for further explanation of Life-world as explained by Schutz.

2-Self-alienation in this context should not be understood in a Marxian fashion but this term has a different resonance within the parameters of Jafarian perspective. Allama Jafari believes that man is neither a purely corporeal being nor a purely ethereal; rather his being represents such an integration which universe in its totality moves toward. Thus self-alienation here signifies the situation within which the man is not conscious of the possibilities of his life as an integral whole (translator).

3 -Adventures of Ideas, p. 33.

profanity, the commercial artists are personally missing the scope of higher moral values and aesthetics this category could dynamically and purposefully offer. Gradual decline or disorder in aesthetic intuition and taste, particularly concerning natural beauties which were once declared very charming in the past is a painful reality. The nature itself and all natural landscapes were so beautiful and attractive that wiped away all bitterness from life and made it more tolerable. A beautiful natural landscape filled human soul with merriment. ["A thing of beauty is a joy forever".][1] Whether the artificial beauties offering kaleidoscopic parade of steels in our mechanical life can offer same relaxation, a beautiful rose or a mountain breeze can offer. Watching electricity come and go has turned off the lights of our pure aesthetic taste that anything could have a lasting sensual charm for us. Though we live under the same blue skies, have same flowers growing around us, and have the same meadows, magnificent mountains and valleys nearby us, but we have forgotten to approach them with fondness and care or to be caressed by them.

Even if I admit that human civilization is expanding while pacing slowly on the path of evolution, why I am unable to feel the same grandeur and magnificence blossoming inside me? Name any society or state, why people are so keen in committing violation of conventions, if everything was going the right way? Unfortunately, every moment of human – the evolutionary being – history is replete with such fraudulent violations of conventions!

1- John Keats: *The Ode to Beauty*.

The Dilemma of Imitation

The promotion of imitation and blind following becomes a live tradition for all wanting to live a physical life, as physical aspects of life seem more natural to them as they happen spontaneously rather than carefully calculated mental life. Such attitude gives rise to certain issues in different domains of culture, which are seven in number[1] and they are discussed below:

First issue: Although "I" live surrounded within multiple environmental and social factors determined by my innate nature, hereditary make up and many other primal factors, I still have a personal feeling about life and I still claim: this is me who lives, enjoys, suffers, endeavors and acts according to the rules and conventions. In short, despite being chained by these determinants, I still feel about my individuality and personal life. Though limiting these factors may never be able to diminish my existence. Provided with this definite observation about personal life, what should 'I' do? Should 'I' continue living 'as it is', i.e. blind following and imitation of others? Such questions have been teasing people along the history of mankind and even by now it continues to be the same so does it seems to continue in the future as well: we inherit personal life style and the will to live from others!

Second issue: My life by no means has been an accident; the fact is evident from countless observations and it can be established with sufficient reasons that after passing through the meander of billions of events in nature, it came to the very position reaching particular time in present. Even if I am not able to answer seven millions of "Whys"

1-For more details see: *A Commentary of Nahj Al-Balaghe*, vol.7/P. 21-22.

that are raised from the very beginning of life, I should have at least one logical interpretation and justification to convince myself to know what is the particular station of my life in this period of human history in context of universal history?

Third issue: What is the ultimate goal (τελος) and acceptable philosophy of life? Except a few number of people across different periods of time, unfortunately all people who pace the course of natural life, decide for their goal and philosophy of life in imitation of others.

Fourth issue: Since I come across numerous styles of life divided into two major kinds: "logically interpretable life" and "unmanageable life torn between natural factors and human desires", which one of these two kinds of life I should choose for me and what premises would make this choice sound rational and logical to others and thus acceptable? Unfortunately, people resort to imitation, following others while choosing between the two approaches to life.

Fifth issue: Are there any places in our world where controversial questions like "where I have come from, why have I come, and where will I go?" could be asked? Yes, there are…. Questioning is permissible … but what about the reasonable answer of these questions? How would they appeal my logic? Alas! Right questions may not deserve the right answers everywhere. Answers can be as stereotyped as the people are tuned in to speak words already mouthed in them. The words just because they are coming out from an individual tongue do not make them original. But who is seeking originality? Doesn't it occur in stark opposition to authority? So why ask any such questions? Unfortunately, denial is met in systematic and most stylish of ways.

Sixth issue: Could we find a way to manage an economic reform that will enable societies to provide more people with staple food produced by people without using any violence, power or deception? Could we reasonably convince those who have achieved such concessions on the basis of their individual talents that: you should use your authority for doing good to yourself and unto other human beings who are in bad need of it? What is the source of designing such reform programs and allowing authorities some concessions to manage such programs? Isn't our choice will remain limited to few known school of thoughts and we may even choose conflicting philosophies to work with the reform policy and its management relying on our personal choice of ideals either selected from our favorite epic or studied in detail during university life.

Seventh issue: Regardless of complete certainty over the order and intelligibility of the world we reside in, we experience sizzling anxiety within ourselves which has very serious foundation. This anxiety stems from (at least) logical possibility of my existential dependence upon the superior being, in fact, the tuner of this giant clock which is called "the world of existence". How could we release ourselves from this anxiety? I cajole and I try to hide, but in vain; unable to deal with it I look for some established source or relieving anxiety physically as others were doing.

Limitations of Naturalism

Sometimes I wonder how our children and youth must be educated that they will be able to live a life free or errors, pure and natural and leading to satiation so that on reaching the last station of life, one does not have to say:

Who am I? A ruined constructionA legend came to its end.

Rather, recalling the adventures of life, one smiles to find all events and states conceived in logic and grown in love.

Unfortunately, "Naturalism" has always been so unclear about the magnificent phenomenon of "liberty"; it has nothing much to say about it but "perfunctorily", something which has unconscious and instinctive realizing, and not something which has some conscious feeling with sacred feelings attached with the phenomenon - liberty. Instead of careful delineation of the phenomenon, the naturalists are content with saying: 'let's go' or 'let's do it'! But that where and how we should go about it is the issue which is irrelevant to commoners and merely belongs to philosophical minds!

The inability of naturalism to establish a logical relationships between provision of foodstuff and human beings in harmony with a free conscience, having taken into consideration all legal concerns and genuine human feelings and emotions has been more lethal than any other aspect. May we claim that imbalanced distribution of resources has caused more dissatisfaction than happiness among people? Every day, we read news about people committing suicide because of poverty. But suicide whether natural or spiritual and its increasing rate would never be surprising for naturalists, since the logic of naturalism interprets the causality in such a way that you could not raise the question: why "self" as an existing thing, provide the cause of its annihilation in itself, without being transformed into a superior "self", or at least, into a different "self" through this annihilation!

Regardless of all common and routinely placed compliments, could we still assert that naturalism has achieved to establish a humanly and logical relationship between the individual and the society? Have not it produced the unnecessary distance between the two – as what is natural for them is what is possible within human body regardless of any cultural values or ethical codes. When no uniformity can be achieved, which can be called society; is there any logic left to call a hound of people 'the society'?[1] The historical observations in this case i.e. examining objectively the stream of life on both sides of the relationship (individuals and society) show that though individual talents and qualities of human beings matter the most, but an individual does not exist in a vacuum, but in context with his social life. When separated, either both of them vanish altogether and/or experience threat of becoming extinct or at least one of them is extremely compromised, when the other tries to tilt balance in its favor alone.

For further illustration of the issue, I'd like to quote **Jean Paul Sartre** with due reservations becauseI am doubtful about its correctness:

Man has history, but not essence!

That is to say, what a person has become qua man is due to what he/she has acquired or learned during the course of life by virtue of his/her social experience and therefore, very naturally it becomes part of history. It is obvious how this phrase reduces the person to social ways of living, without giving any room to those human qualities which could be realized in other open societies, subsequently, buries the individual in the cemetery of history. The problem is: what should be done so that the realization of human talents in the context of social life does not to lead to the obliteration of talents, liberties, and genuine feelings and emotions. The answer does not apparently lie in a meager logical relationship between the individual and the society. It seems that human history itself witnesses to the fact that most of the complaints of

---

1-If people can be brute and selfish like animals, there is no harm calling them pack of wolves or hound of jackals. (editor)

intelligent people had had their origin in their ignorance of the secrets of existence, but my concern here is that: does it seem sensible at all to kick the person with enormous talents and individual qualities to a side view amidst several hundreds of other valuable figures, and punish him/her by assigning first homo-social forms and then bury them alive in the cemetery of history?

For example, could **Abuzar Ghafari**[1] be reduced to merely environmental and social factors, while historical facts all witness to his noble personality as an intelligent figure? Could **Socrates**, with all his noble individual qualities, be reduced to a historical event celebrating a cup of hemlock? Is modern philosophical mind more developed than that of ancient **Aristotle**? Are the brains of modern geometricians and mathematicians more developed than that of **Euclid**? Do our minds today work more logical than that of **Abu-Reyhan Biruni, Avicenna, Ibn Khaldun** and **Jalaladdin Muhammad Molawi(Rumi)**to demonstrate the existence of life-world for **Berkeley**?

Has naturalism been successful in defining the boundaries of the prohibited area of human souls?

Since the naturalism allows unrestrained and fierce competition between human beings grounded in the slogan raised by **Thomas Hobbes e.g.**: "Man is a wolf to his fellow man". Blind following of such ideas definitely prepares the workforce which is ready to exhaust any amount of mental and physical energies in the name of cut-throat competition, to overcome illusory barriers and to have blood bath in victory. Therefore, hardly any time is left for leisure activities – to develop a Philosophy of life, to set goals and envisage programs

---

1-One of distinguished disciples of Prophet Muhammad (peace be upon him).

to achieve them; above all to use one's mental and physical energies wisely to understand "Intelligible Life and the paths leading to it".

Since the scientific evidence gathered by naturalism supports all ideas of taking advantage of physical and mental energies for organizing corporeal aspects of human existence, at its best, it can charge enthusiasm for ordinary habits like eating, sleeping, manipulating anger, greed and lust in oneself or the others. It can hardly ever move beyond or go in pursuit of higher perfection seeking values. Those who are following 'Natural life style' live their lives in a kind of mechanical stupor ordained over them, which they can hardly overcome to wake up and arrange some food for their hungry souls. Therefore, the harbingers of "Naturalism" have to forge some absolute unconditional truths for their hungry intelligences in order to quench their thirst for absolute perfection with these pure mental abstractions.

One of the very evident peculiarities of "Naturalism" has always been that they tend to lay the foundation of their life and careers in competition with other fellows, a competition which is hard or made to look like one, giving rise to a feeling of overcoming a natural obstacle, thus having an excuse for any responsibility of the misdeeds, thus committed, or own the natural causality in oneself, because after all it was not a humane situation dealing with humans. Thinkers like **Herbert Spencer**, however, pronounce in complete peace of mind that: man in his historical movement pace on the path of evolution! It would be no longer surprising to hear that: the more fatal is the competition of an individual or a group of individuals with his/their fellow men, the more competent he/they seem to be for the title of hero! This is also another reason for the correctness of the slogan that: man is pacing on the path of rational evolution!

It is far from any doubt that intelligent anthropologists and philanthropists have nothing to say about the prevalence of lie, both in simple and complex forms, in human societies but: this is exactly the pure natural life as you can see for yourself! Since it has no objective but expanding the dominion of "natural self" throughout all human and natural realities, natural life takes advantage of all realities whatsoever to satisfy natural desires of natural self. This is why "right and wrong", "true and false", "good and bad", "ugly and beautiful", "good and evil" and "I" in general and its proper relationship with "*Nicht-Ich*" have no place in the domain of "natural life", whereas, these dichotomies, which pertain to different types of human relationship with the world and fellow men, have their roots in human nature.

Pathology of Satisfaction

It is said: humanity is satisfied only by leading purely a natural life, which of course resides in pursuit of physical growth of one's body, realizing all bodily needs emerging in body in context of any personal or social situation. That is why this style has been selected by the majority of people during all periods of history as dominant way of life. They have been moving in the sphere of "Naturalism" to meet their personal-social needs in life. Such a claim suffices naturalists claim that it is not the best but the only way to live this earthly life.

I may agree with their claim that most of people move within the borders of physical needs of life, but we should never consider the satisfaction proclaimed and movement thus achieved as an outcome of living in such a way, because for me it is neither simple nor natural as understood by many. If we look more closely, we will find that: the professed satisfaction and the movement are a direct effect of "*Philautia* (self-love)" which is called "*Conatus* (self-protection)", "autonomy" and according to some biologists: "self-assurance". And this wholesome self-love and self-concern, the main characteristics of living beings in fact stems from the biological instinct of survival, where one is pushed to take care of one self. Thus, it is the cause and not the outcome of living naturally, where the major concern is always to fulfill one's physical needs. The social needs that fall in this sphere and become a compulsion are also those, which are related to the survival in group, because humans are essentially gregarious beings. That is to say, the satisfaction is rather imposed – a compulsion - rather than a natural outcome of a life style. Unfortunately, common people assume this satisfaction to be in complete agreement with the gamut of human talents and possibilities – something which was natural and not earned. Further detailed and close examination of 'satisfactions' achieved tell us story about underlying reasons, which could be unveiled, such as:

1. The satisfaction resulted from lacking a strong will and inability to bear any change in current state of affairs that is established upon the gratification of some of desires and the absence of some of hardships.
2. The satisfaction resulting from being released from the pressures and anxieties that disrupt natural life and make it cumbersome. If such satisfaction prevails in life, it entails needing more and more energy to exhaust to release the weariness and boredom resulting from continuous evasion of the pressures and anxieties of natural life.
3. The satisfaction resulting fromthe preordained environmental and social factors, either these factors cause the disappearance of some of human existential constituents

or add some others to them, since it is always taken for granted that the preordained environmental and social factors would oblige the person to surrender, and one would not be able to pinpoint the reason for submission unable to establish cause and effect links. If this person has enough potential to envisage a higher level of life than naturalism, he would content himself with a "sigh" but if he has not enough potential to do so, in fear of losing the satisfaction, he would argue that higher level of life in a way that he may not find himself a loser being unable to touch it. The common and distressing peculiarity of this naive and primitive satisfaction, which is indoctrinated, whether consciously or unconsciously, by the maxim "life has always been so, and is just right so", helps in holding back people from touching the magnificence of higher echelons of life. If only once his eyes are to be partially lightened up with beacon of the higher levels of life, he will acknowledge them in reference to the paradigms and principles of naturalism, he is in habit of attributing his satisfaction to, and he will conclude in despondence that: it is not really worthy enough to leave the current state of affairs which satisfy me.

Personal satisfaction constructs such a strong defense, an impenetrable barrier in front of their reasons which hinders their rational activities and thus doesn't allow them to understand that: the very recognition and assessment of the current state of affairs and reaching an intelligible satisfaction is not possible without transcending existing state of affairs. Indeed, they will never understand the mantra:

> I became water, while seeing myself but a mirageI became a sea, while seeing myself but a bubbleI became conscious,

while seeing but my ignoranceI became awaken, while seeing myself but steeped in slumber.[1]

Another peculiarity of this naive satisfaction is gradual returning to ignorance and lassitude, and exhausting life in fruitless challenges with whatever we may find as "bothersome". There is a wide gap between this naive satisfaction and "Intelligible Life" according to which: the sameness of two days in someone's life is a great loss for him?

4. The satisfaction results from the pleasure we get from fulfilling our physical wants in life. Having understood life as "seeking pleasure as much as possible and keeping oneself away from pains and disturbances", **Epicureans**, whether consciously or unconsciously, have such a conception of satisfaction. Such seekers of satisfaction would soon experience loss, because of the inherent flaw in their basic conception, understanding man as a being in vacuum and the consequent belief that human pleasures and pains are accidental happenings. They are blind to the fact that most of the hedonic pleasures are consequence of sadism, inflicting incessant pain, tortures and disturbances on others to stay happy oneself, as **Nāser Khōsrō** says:

Ten men must sleep with pale faces and hungrySo you could make your face rosaceous with red wine.

These despicable people never would come to touch the reality that joining others in their sorrows and grief, when a possibility exists to personally avoid them, just for the sake of unity in life – which is the manifestation of providence – is more valuable and magnificent than seeking personal

---

1-These verses are allegedly by **Binava Badakhshani.**

pleasures. Satisfaction with personal pleasures, which are contrived at body and not heart, is the primary and fundamental characteristic of naturalism, one of the impenetrable barriers that block the way between the people and "intelligible life". I wish Epicurus would have contented himself with his atomistic theory of the origin of natural things; doing so he might not have slowed down human movement by providing authenticity to hedonism with his theories.

5. Natural satisfactions havealways been obstacles in the way of human movement toward personal independence and freedom. Satisfaction in itself, however, is counted as one of the most wonderful individual and social phenomenon, which has unfortunately always been partially discussed.

There are only a few people indeed in every society who could indulge in continuous examination of existing satisfactions through a logical analysis of their intentions, motives, resulting behaviors and their impact. This is the reason that people remain busy and exhaust most of their mental and physical energies to remove obstacles in their day to day life, instead of taking advantage, and realizing such opportunities for understanding the life itself and finding true happiness in "intelligible life" the passionate desire for which is deeply rooted inside them.

Let us not speak anymore about the shameful fact that how this deteriorated concept of naturalism has ruined useful and constructive powers of people just to establish its own hegemony, the protagonists of naturalism have been monopolizing the power to their advantage and still flatter themselves by rejoicing on the ignorance of common man and playing willfully with their predatory habit. Being predator is being natural; more natural is to combat the predator. Where this battle will take place – On physical grounds or on mental grounds? The choice lies with us - the people belonging to so called knowledge age.

6. Satisfaction is such a phenomenon that is always mistaken for "the sense of freedom" and thus when someone finds oneself satisfied with a given condition misperceives him/her at complete freedom. Only, if one could deeply analyze that satisfaction, I wonder, how much dissatisfaction and displeasure one may find with that satisfaction. Even if this analyzer is partially conscious, he will understand very soon that: having enjoyed that naive satisfaction, in every condition of life, he has just flattered himself with an illusion - disguised coercion in the name of self-independence and freedom. Let's have a closer look on some instances of satisfaction:

a. Maulana Rumi narrates in **Mathnavi'e Ma'navi** [Spiritual Couplets], the example of a fly perched on a floating straw in urine of a donkey sees itself the victorious captain of a vessel sailing on vast ocean heading it toward the shore:

> A fly in donkey's urine, perched on straw,Just like a boatman gazing at the shore,Said, 'Straw and urine are my boat and sea,I've contemplated this fact recently:I'm in the sea, the captain of my boat,Following maps and methods learned by rote.'In urine it would steer its straw-made raftAs if in boundless seas, for it was daft:It thought a single drop could stretch so farUnable to observe things as they are,Its world stretched out as far it could view,Small eyes count as a sea a drop or two!

> Narrow interpreters are like this fly,With straw and urine they all falsifyIf you stop reading from your own small view,The phoenix will grant kingdoms then to you!Still,

those who've worked this out aren't really flies,Spirits don't correspond to body-size.[1]

[In this analogy Maulana has described the true worth of the ordinary and profane ambitions of the people who seek satisfaction by falling from grace. It always remains indignant and shallow and cannot be compared with the spiritual satisfaction of some higher achievement.]

b. Imagine a bunch of frogs that leave their small lake at dusk for the riverside and after staying there for a short while, they come back to their small lake by night and suddenly find shiny points on the surface of limpid water of the lake and they ask each other overwhelmed with amazement: what are these things which have occupied our lake after we left? They have entered our home without permission. Frogs clamorously declare war on them: let's clear them all out of our home. They all jump in the lake over their targets and strike the shiny points with their little hands and feet. Little ripples created by the jump temporarily scramble the picture of shiny points on water. Thus, a sense of satisfaction embraces the frogs as if they have conquered the world – at least freed their territory from aliens. Do you know what these shiny points were? They were the reflections of stars from our galaxy abound with numerous celestial bodies.[2]

c. Children's satisfaction with their war and peace:

1-Mathnai'e Ma'navi, book I.

2-This anecdote is by**Illia Abu-Maz**i, the renowned Lebanese poet.

Their war and peace are based on fantasyand shame and pride are both illusory.[1]

d. The satisfaction of the tanner with the smells of tannery who fainted when he entered the bazaar of perfumers. Everyone came up with a diagnosis and tried a remedy, until a wise man asked: what is the trade of this man? After much inquiry, it was known that his vocation is tanning of dirty leathers. He recommended them to take the tanner to his tannery. They did so, and then the tanner was cured:

> *He that was born in the stove and never saw purity, the smell of musk produces a painful effect upon him.*

> *A certain man fell senseless and curled up as soon as he came into the bazaar of the perfumers.The scent of the perfume (floating) from the goodly perfumers smote him, so that his head reeled and he fell on the spot.*

> *He fell unconscious, like a carcass, at noontide in the middle of the thorough-fare.Thereupon the people gathered over him, all crying la hawl and applying remedies.One was putting his hand on his (the tanner s) heart, while another sprinkled rose-water upon him;(For) he did not know that from (smelling) rose-water in the meadow (the bazaar) that calamity had overtaken him.*

> *One was massaging his hands and head, and another was bringing moist clay mixed with straw (to serve as a cold plaster).*[2]

1-Mathnai'e Ma'navi, book I.

2- Ibid: book IV.

e. The satisfaction of masses, unenlightened peoplewith their feeling of personal freedom: "I do whatever I want, and no rule could stop me", their much enthusiasm for action regardless of consequences always turns out to be a trap for their lifetime imprisonment craving for bodily satisfaction. Maulana Rumi has commented in Mathnavi that a bird is always trapped by listening to sweet tunes of the hunter and overlooking the net laid on ground which will hold them tied to ground, never they would be able to sail freely in skies now. After all, what the birds cared for – just a morsel of bread to satisfy hunger?[1]

Realizing all painful dilemmas previously discussed, it remains doubtful, whether or not pursuit of physical life leads to desired satisfaction or not? But the people have become so dull in their perception that they want to remain in illusion of satisfaction rather than coming out of their intoxicated state to face reality.

1-Mathnai'e Ma'navi, book I.

Chapter Two

The Fundamentals of Intelligible Life

This chapter discusses the basics of the alternative life-style suggested by Allama Muhammad Taghi Jafari to get an integrated concept of life and living and broadening the scope of commoners to take the course to intellectual evolution. Allama has slowly and gradually build the awareness of alternative style – the intelligible life, while creating a strong desire to have it. The chapter is divided into following sections:

1. Intelligible life -an Integrated Conception of Life
   - ✓ *Why Intelligible Life?*

2. Quran and Intelligible Life
   - ✓ *Quranic Views about Satisfaction*

3. The Definition of Intelligible Life
   - ✓ *The Meaning of "Intelligible" in "Intelligible Life"*

4. Reason and Reasoning
   - ✓ *The Definition of Reason*
   - ✓ *Using Reason*
   - ✓ *Kinds of Human Reason*

5. Rumi's Criticism on Speculative Reason

6. Using Speculative Reason in Intelligible Life

7. Intelligible Life and Rationalism

Intelligible life – an IntegratedConception of Life

After reviewing the philosophy of "naturalism" and characteristics of living merely a physical life and itsnatural outcomes, I'd like to shift my focus unto the study *"Intelligible Life"*.

To begin with, it is worth noting that study of life styles is not happening for the first time; neither this debate about choice of life styles has been started by us, nor our arguments will end it. Human social living has been very interesting topic of investigation; many brilliant minds, both in past and in present, have probed deeply in this significant phenomenon using logical analysis and/or synthesis of various perspectives and point of views to understand and explain the phenomenon and some have succeeded to find answers for the hard core problems faced in this field. We acknowledge and commend all sincere efforts done in the past and we wish the same success for all thinkers undertaking this divine enterprisein future. We also know that the empirical and the intellectual contributions made by these thinkers havebeen invaluable in development of social sciences and humanities, ignoring for the moment, the intangible influence of some prefabricated ideas in their judgments.

No doubt that the debate of "intelligible life" is possible in all domains of social, psychological and anthropological studies encompassing human life. Presently, we feel that studying 'intelligible life" more thoroughly is of vital significance; therefore, we keenly endeavor to engage in our lively discussion the mature and powerful minds who have participated in this cautious debate of liberating human minds and souls from the carefree attitude of naturalists. We intend to approach the topic, "intelligible life" in such an implicit and exclusive fashion so that we can avoid adding pain to human consciousness which is already sick and tired of rapid transitions from one physical state to another, procuring one satisfaction and proclaiming the other; rather then we will beseech a sublime transformation from want of physical life to a more natural demand of an "intelligible life".

Why Intelligible Life?

I would like to begin the discussion on our main topic "intelligible life" with discussion on the principle of consequentialism, as understood by philosophers and as stated by Holy Quran. Whenever, we talk about choice of behaviors, it entails the study of consequentialism.[1] Cultures are distinguished by their individual habits of dealing with pains and pleasures and understanding their moral underpinning, such as Buddha quoted law of Karma and Quran states law of recompense. This process of selecting and de-selecting or valuing certain behaviors and despising others depends upon human understanding of the causes and implications of certain behaviors. Thus, by implying their distinguished taste in choice people define the anthropology of their respective cultures. So let us begin the rubric of this debate by discussing some popular views of sociologists and anthropologists that will culminate at citation of verses from Holy Quran which are concerned with "intelligible life".

1-Consequentialism is the philosophical approach, which implies that people choose different behaviors because of their moral consequences. According to many psychologists such as Sigmund Freud, the choice depends upon pleasure principle, i.e. human beings tend to seek pleasures and avoid pains. Consequentialism has led to the foundation of Modern moral Philosophy, with theories such as hedonism and utilitarianism setting people in action. The term "consequentialism" was coined by G. E. M. Anscombe in her essay "Modern Moral Philosophy" in 1958, to describe what she saw as the central error of certain moral theories, such as those propounded by John Stuart Mill and Henry Sidgwick (editor).

The consequential principle as defined by social anthropologists is the delicate concomitance between two propositions of "human life is so" and "human life ought to be so" that is sorely disregarded by most of the scholars in humanities. Without realizing this delicate concomitance our ontological and anthropological research would probably encounter many difficulties. We could never dictate any "ought" to the world of laws and determine its relationship with constituents while interpreting or explaining it.

For instance, our knowledge of water as a compound, composed of Oxygen and Hydrogen, doesn't result in saying O' water! Your composition is right, keep it so. Or O' water! Your composition is wrong, change it fast! Water will remain the water forever and nothing could change its essential nature by dictating any imperative to it. Contrarily, when a scholar in humanities develops a theory about the nature of life and human mental characteristics, all human beings take a stand toward it: this theory characterize me so, now whether I should endorse it in myself or refute it? What impact its acceptance or refutation will have upon "me"?

That is why we say: if we don't have thinkers who could provide us with the best interpretation and justification of super-unity of life through harmonizing "the life as it is" and "life as ought to be", we would have no hope for removing the obstacles in the way of rational and mental evolution and thus, no solution for reducing the devastating pains. As a matter of fact, life is not like a brickbat outside human nature, so that we could distinguish between its "is-ness" and "ought-ness"; however, if we could manage the brickbat by reaching deep down to its essence, we may shape it in any desired form, but life is such a phenomenon within which "the subject and the object", "the perceiver and the perceived", "the dominant and the dominated" and "the constructive and the constructed" are all unified. There is no place for such experimentation for fun!

We could pursue fun and fantasy in imaginary poems, but what about trying to establish serious understanding of the phenomenon of life? When a living man says that he is a slave of predestined factors, not only does he express a reality "as it is", but he implicitly implants the idea in his mind that I am the slave of predestined factors. On the contrary, when he says that man is a free being, he insinuates that I am free. It may sound practical for the common people, but how do these commoners reach such perceptions, but through words enunciated by the pioneers of knowledge of human society and culture?

John Stuart Mill, in his writings, hasnot only illustrated "man as he is" through explaining manifold domains of human freedom (the liberty that people can enjoy from choosing within a hierarchy of pleasures, some carnal and some ephemeral), but in doing so he implicitly depicts "man as he ought to be" (what are the preferred choices in comparison with natural ones). In a similar way, when determinists, like **Spinoza** or cybernetic researchers, say: "this is the man", they also indirectly allude to "man as he ought to be".

Generally speaking, it seems that every thinker who suggests an idea of human life "as it is", particularly when he is a distinguished academic figure, he willy-nilly suggests an idea about "the man as he ought to be", in absolute regard of the principle of realism that exists in the very nature of human being. Therefore, suggesting any idea of "the man as he is" implies taking him along the path of "oughtness".

Taking into deep consideration, principles discussed above, the necessity of harmony between two issues of "is" and "ought" in human life becomes obvious (the lesser, the gap between "is" and "ought", the lesser is the confusion in human ideas leading towards harmonious culture. Contrarily, the more is the gap, more skeptic human thought is and increasing are the conflicts disrupting cultural development). Our studies have shown us there is no way but "Intelligible Life" to reach this harmony.

Only within the paradigm of intelligible life we could well interpret and justify the privileged potential of human kind and successfully engage in handling with their rational and psychological barriers.

Quran and Intelligible Life

I'd like to begin the discussion of intelligible life with citations of some verses from the Holy Quran:

> *...that he who would perish might perish by clear proof, and he who would live might live by clear proof...*[1]

> *You who believe! Answer (the call of) Allah and his messenger when he calls you to that which gives you life.*[2]

It is well evident that this verse has addressed people living at that time in history and not the dead people rotten in their graves. However, the "death" alludes to the 'dead consciousness' as their life was nothing but reduced to some bestial autonomic movements (satisfaction of basic instincts). Therefore, such people are pronounced dead, the ones who had nothing of life but a name. Thus, the life that Islam has invited all of us to lead is the "Intelligible Life".

> *Whoever does good whether male or female and he is a believer, we will most certainly make him live a happy life [that is, Intelligible Life].*[3]
> *Allah confirms those who believe with the sure word in this world's life and in the hereafter...*[4]

1- Al-Anfal: 42.

2- Al-Anfal: 24.

3- Al-Nahl: 97.

4- Ibrahim: 27.

The essential demand of "intelligible life" resides in principle that human reason trained in morality governs human life and must endeavor to seek evolutionary unity of life, and people in this pursuit will conserve moral uprightness of their character, regardless of their mundane choices of individual behaviors in their life. This stability and cohesion is not possible without being guided and commanded by moral reason.

> *Surely my prayer and my sacrifice and my life and my death*
> *are (all) for Allah, the lord of the worlds.*[1]

Nothing but "intelligible life" would satisfy God. The life swamped with carnal and satanic desires based on greedy chase of power and autocracy could not be associated with the Creator who has ordained us to abstain from such a way of life and He has blessed us with rational logic, conscience, prophets and saints to remain on the right path.

Quranic Views about Satisfaction

Holy Quran does not relish that people should spend their lives in pursuit of mundane physical pleasures and ignore their subtle reality of a spiritual and knowledge being. Quran has warned people to abstain from such primitive and naïve means of satisfaction, as have been discussed in previous section. Quran proclaims its preferences in different verses such as:

1)**Are you contented with this world's life instead of the hereafter?**[2]Undoubtedly, "this world's life" implies granted physical life of a specific tenure which is in sharp contrast with Quranic concept of "pure life" or "reasonable life" (the life which is based on clear proof) as stated in following verse: "**And he**

1- Al-Ana'm: 162.
2- Al-Tawba: 38.

who would live might live by clear proof; and most surely Allah hearing, knowing".[1] The clear proof or evidence is definite given in revealed books or lives of Prophets and celebrate personalities of religions.

2) **And whenever a chapter is revealed, saying: believe in Alla and strive hard along with his messenger, those having ampleness means ask permission of you and say: leave us (behind), that we ma be with those who sit* They preferred to be with those wl remained behind, and a seal is set on their hearts so they do n understand* But the messenger and those who believe with hi strive hard with their property and their persons; and these it is wl shall have the good things and these it is who shall be successful.**[2]

As stated in these verses, some people are stuck wit satisfaction related to material accomplishments in life, such a property, wealth and power; they prefer to give up any effo for good deeds (intelligible life) requiring sacrifices of the material belongings, so that their physical comfort continge upon their luxurious worldly life is not disturbed. In Rumi words: "I don't want eye, make me blind fast"! Here is the cle proof: people seeking ordinary pleasures seal their hearts ar shut their minds for protection of "material life".

3) **Surely those who do not hope in our meeting and are pleas with this world's life and are content with it, and those who a heedless of our verses* (As for) those, their abode is the fire becau of what they earned.**[3]

While contemplating on these verses, we realize th satisfaction with earthly life and having confidence that it w last forever and becoming heedless of divine truth of death ar the life hereafter, one step follows the other. In the light of th

---

1- Al-Anfal: 42.
2- Al-Tawba: 86-88.

argument, the relationship between such states of mind, whether they are the causality, simultaneity or merely a coincidence, is conjured to turn oneself away from "pure" and "reasonable" life (the life which is based on clear proof) – synonymous to "intelligible life". Thus, we might say that having no hope for direct meeting with God and being contented with physical life granted on earth, disregarding principles of life coded in divine verses, all these attitudes are in stark opposition with the phenomenon - "intelligible life" – the worthiest, hence the most natural object of desire for human beings.

Instead of seeking the primitive and naive bodily satisfactions which is the characteristic of being inclined to "natural life", Holy Quran has proposed a superior satisfaction which arises from developing a taste for "intelligible life" (the life which is based on clear proof), and realize it as the consequence of mature souls in direct communication with God:

> O' soul that art at rest!* return to your lord, well-pleased (with him), well-pleasing (him),* so enter among my servants,* and enter into my garden.[1]

The tranquility – peace of mind – which according to above-mentioned verses is the prerequisite for returning to the God is such peace of heart that enables the person to face God and to enlist oneself among His chosen servants. This tranquility arises from active steps taken towards self-actualization, and it is not achieved by remaining swamped with deceptive desires of natural life which are satisfied only through hardships and misfortunes labeled by constant realization that other people

---

1- Al-Fajr: 27-30.

are doing better than us. Isn't it a disguised torment for human conscience that may kill it or deteriorate it to anti-conscience?

The fact that we must strive to establish "intelligible life" is an essential human necessity established historically, and not merely a utopian ideal, that should be realized despite passing waves of multifarious consolations and self-deceptions which were met on the way of natural life, and so were justified. This passionate call for intelligibility does not sound only from the East, the cradle of civilization, but there are Western humanist philosophers and scholars like **Alfred North Whitehead** who profess that:

> We stand at a moment when the course of history depends
> upon the calm reasonableness arising from a religious public
> opinion.[1]

The Definition of Intelligible Life

Having taken into consideration all positive and constructive characteristics of humanity in general and examining objective consequences of following animalistic life by human beings throughout history, sensing the ardent enthusiasm of intellectuals and conscientious people in different cultures, and recalling the sayings of great human minds of history; we could define "intelligible life" as follows:

Intelligible life is:

> A conscious life which canalizes deterministic and pseudo-
> deterministic forces and activities of natural life into the
> course of relative evolutionary goals through the development
> of liberty which flourishes in human will as it would assist

---

1-Adventures of Ideas (1961): p 19.

human self, which is gradually developed in this process, to realize the Ultimate Telos of Life, i.e. participation in general cosmic movement toward Supreme Perfection.

After reaching a simple but concise definition of "intelligible life", I'd like to proceed with the discussion of relevant issues concerned with leading such a way of life.

The Meaning of "Intelligible" in "Intelligible Life"

Some people may confuse the meaning of *"intelligible"* with speculative use of reason, which has been aggressively criticized by intellectuals, scholars, and mystics of the East and the West. Some thinkers may assume that the method used to arrive at "intelligible life" will essentially be Western rationalism. To clearly and objectively manifest the meaning of *"intelligible"*, we begin with succinct definition of reason followed by a concise interpretation and classification of reason [intellect][1] and reasoning [intellection].[2]

1- Reason is the human faculty which distinguishes human beings from other beings. Reason empowers us to "choose"; i.e. to select for us when a number of choices are available, e.g., to speak the truth, when one could have lied easily. It implies the capacity of interpretation and analysis, of comparing and contrasting, and of looking at similarities while examining objects, persons, situations and various phenomenon of nature. The more efficient the use of reason is; the more intelligent a person is considered (editor).

2-The use of reason is called reasoning or intellection. It can vary in its potential from person to person, since it needs coaching and development. It can vary in its nature and complexity as well depending upon the subject matter under discussion (editor).

Reason and Reasoning

The Definition of Reason

All of us are well aware of the fact that human brain has the ability to operate multiple activities at a time, with each set of activities having its own origin, mechanism, significance and outcomes at individual or group level. Some activities are related with regulation of bodily functions, such as respiration and digestion, while others are related to human thoughts and emotions. We label each set of these activities by conceptualization, i.e. assigning defining terms to these set of activities. Reaching these definitions not only sets limits and scope to the idea but we are also able to distinguish one set of ideas from the other.

Taking for instance two terms,'association of ideas' and 'exaggeration', association of ideas refers to: linking together various units or propositions, which seem to share either formal similarities, or measureable cause and effect relationship in a spatio-temporal context, or any other perceived meaningful relationship. However, instead of using such detailed and lengthy explanation we sum up our ideas in just two words: *association of ideas*. After assigning this term we are assured that this mental activity (*association of ideas*) will always be understood and used in this meaningful context and it will notbe confused with other mental activities, say for example with 'exaggeration' which is also a mental activity but entails deletion and selection of certain facts from objective reality, the acceptance of "nothing" as "absolute" or vice versa, followed by the state of being impressed by the act of deletion of some facts and selection and acceptance of others, intensifying the impression that the real picture of facts might have given rise to, like those exaggerations that happen in stage drama and cinemascreen.

However,reason and reasoning [or intellect and intellection] are not such determinate notions as *'association of ideas'* and *'exaggeration'*, since there are many mental activities that are classified under the category of reasoning: e.g.

1) There is an activity in brain that chooses a goal among probable goals.
2) There is another activity in brain which selects appropriate means for reaching the goal. These two activities are both called "reasoning" and they both are done by "reason".

Types of Reasoning

Reasoning is divided into two broad categories: i) scientific, ii) practical.The scientific reasoning functions through such logical devices as definitions, explanations, logical syllogisms, empirical inductions and so on implying what is a person's belief; how does one establish a cause and effect relationship in a given situation, whereas, Practical kind of reasoning implies the choice of action to reach the goal and careful selection of appropriate means to reach a given goal, as discussed by Aristotle in his theory of 'praxis'.

Using Reason

1) **Mental abstraction:**It implies nullification of individual characteristics and objective determinations of realities. It is also part of reasoning and is either done quantitatively, such as abstracting numbers from objectively numbered things and/or qualitatively by abstracting universals from objectively observed particulars.

   It is noted here that abstraction is not limited only to the mental activity of abstracting the quantity from phenomena but it may involve abstraction of communalities among genre of a particular genus or a species as well. The process of abstraction could be hierarchical, like step by step abstracting several universal numbers out of a given number and in turn regard the universals thus achieved as numbered objects, such as one universal, two universal, three universal, four universal and so forth. Similarly categorizing of some universals as particulars, while accepting them as universals but at the same time expecting to abstract more particulars from them, like abstracting genus from species.

2) Use of reason has also been specified as the regulator of emotions and physical urges, on one hand, and of religious, moral and social rules, on the other.

3) Using reason has also been regarded mandatory while coordinating inner and outer world for a proper positioning of individual in context of the whole stream of life.

4) Using reason has also been prescribed as the chief discriminator between "right and wrong" and "true and false".

Kinds of Reason

Philosophers, theosophists and spiritual mystics, both in East and West, have divided reason into three kinds:

I) Speculative reason that has also been termed as pure or theoretical reason implies the use of deductive logic creating the argument for *"as it is"*. This type of reasoning has frequently been criticized by moralists like Aquinas and Kant or mystics like Jalaladin Muhammad Molawi (Rumi).

II) Practical reason that implies use of conscience with a sufficient knowledge of values within a specific culture. Such reasoning involves choice of action, decision, and particulars which are applicable in a particular case. Philosophers like Aquinas and Kant have built their Philosophy around development and use of this kind of reasoning.

III) Universal reason or Divine Intellect that is a manifestation of "The Reason of Universe". This type of intuitive reasoning has been used by spiritual and mystical philosophers like [Ibn-Arabi and] Rumi.[1]

After understanding the nature of reason and kinds of reasoning, the explanation of the *"intelligible"* in "Intelligible Life" becomes easy. One thing is sure that *"intelligible"* in "Intelligible Life" does not imply the speculative reason, since speculation only offers systematic ordering of particular premises through scientific thinking to reach the goals without paying attention to other existing realities of human life. Speculative reason abstracts numbers and sets up symbols, and works best in developing mathematical logic in domain of natural sciences. Speculative reasoning provides us with the empirical evidence, but it does not provide any hint, whether this mathematical operation or inference will be used for the best interest of the researcher and other human beings or not? Thus, it is considered a primary step in the hierarchy of rational development occupied mostly with physical nuances of the subject matter under study.

When the objectives described are separated from their intended outcomes, i.e. separating means from the end, how

---

1-In Greek Philosophy the term is understood as "Nous", kind of an intuitive capacity or spiritual intelligence. Similarly, in Islamic Philosophy the intellection is understood as the process of connecting one's intelligence with the divine intelligence, as defined by Avicenna (see History of Islamic Philosophy by Nasr & Leaman), who endorsed this intellectual mechanism, as way of using one's reason beyond the use of five senses, to try to understand the logic of creation and the system of universe. The process of intellection leads to the initiation of inner eye of mind or "Qalb" bringing spiritual transformation in one's life as propounded by Rumi and others, when one is able to see the physical craft, and the moral logic behind creation of universe. Thus the vision of the creator and the created becomes one. This spiritual unification helps the human to carry out the divine mission designated for Life and the living as implied by Mulla Sadra in his transcendent theosophy or Al Jilli in explaining Universal Man – Insaan-i-Kaamil (editor).

could people get benefited from the strategies framed by calculated logical inferences? Therefore, it becomes very hard to internalize and own such logics. Though these personally constructed logics appear to coordinate between individual aspirations, emotions and motivations on one hand and social and/or religious morality on the other, somehow they choose to remain silent on the authenticity of their choice whether this coordination is right or not. Being essentially theoretical, it can well explain ways of restoring the internal and external balance that is deteriorated by a particular problem, but it does not offer any practical judgment, especially when dealing with moral or ethical dilemmas leading to political conflicts rooted in right-winged politics limiting human liberty and freedom to take necessary action. We may summarize our conclusion in following points that speculative reason has two distinctive functions:

1- Explaining "what is" by analysis and/or synthesis.

2- Gearing people towards their recognized goal through objective means in realist terms but lacking in moral justification for its relevance with other aspects of life.

Rumi's Criticism on Speculative Reason

The very doubt on the legitimacy of using certain logics, "speculative reason" has been severely criticized in many stories narrated in *Spiritual Couplets of Rumi*; Maulana advocates limited use of such reasoning, especially when we deal in world of human emotions. Some of such verses are cited below:

> *This intellect does not pass beyond a grave and sepulcher,and this (intellectual) foot does not tread the arena of marvels.*

> *Go; become quit of this foot and this intellect: seek the eye appertaining to the invisible (the inward eye) and enjoy (contemplation).*

How should one subservient to a preceptor and in pupilage to a book   find, like Moses, light from (his own) bosom?

From this (scholastic) study and this intellect comes naught but vertigo; therefore leave this study and adopt (in its stead) expectation.

Do not seek (spiritual) eminence from disputation: for him who is expectant (of Divine inspiration) listening is better than speaking.

The office of teaching is a sort of sensual desire: every sensual fancy is an idol (source of polytheism) in the Way.

If every busybody had found the track (had attained) to His grace, how should God have sent so many prophets?

The particular intellect is like the lightning and the flash: how is it possible to go to Wakhsh in a flash?

The light of the lightning is not for guidance on the way; nay, it is a command to the cloud to weep.

The lightning of our intellect is for the sake of weeping, to the end that non-existence may weep in longing for (real) existence.

The child s intellect said, "Attend school"; but it cannot learn by itself.

The sick man's intellect leads him to the physician; but his intellect is not successful in curing him.[1]

* * *

Thou strive much, and at last even thou thyself sayest in weariness that the intellect is a fetter.[2]

* * *

The false (discursive) reason, indeed, sees the reverse (of the truth): it sees life as death, O man of weak judgements."[1]

1-Mathnai'e Ma'navi, book IV: 3312-3323.
2-Ibid: 3353.

* * *

He (God) made the intellect a reader of those figured characters, that thereby He might put an end to its contrivances.[2]

* * *

Come into the river (of reality), dash the pitcher (of phenomenal form) against the stone, set fire to (mere) scent and colour.[3]

* * *

His soul has never known the delight of (spiritual) freedom: the chest of (phenomenal) forms is his arena.

His mind is forever imprisoned in forms: he (only) passes from cage into cage.[4]

* * *

Love is reckless, not Reason: Reason seeks that from which it may get some profit.[5]

* * *

The intellect is strong in the head but weak in the legs, because it is sick of heart (spiritually decayed) though sound of body (materially flourishing).[6]

There are numerous verses written in the same spirit in *Love Poems of Rumi* as well where he has continued with his tradition of criticizing over-use and misuse of speculative reason.

O' my son! Reason does only hinder the wayfarerSo don't listen to it the way is just clear.

1-Ibid: book V: 1764.

2-Ibid: 316.

3-Ibid: 4081.

4-Ibid: book VI: 4510-4511.

5-Ibid: 1967.

6-Ibid: 119.

When individual human reason only hinders the wayfarers, the heart becomes deceptive and the soul works as a veil, because the speculative reason has already ruined the heart and the soul:[1]

> *O' my son! Reason hinders, Heart deceives and Soul veilsThe way is closed to these three all.*

After being imprisoned by speculative reason, one could hardly expect to experience true love – the sesame of existence:

> *O' my son! Love is not the task of tender-hearted peopleLove is the task of a hero.*

This idea has been represented in one verse of *The Lyrics of Hafiz*as follows:

> *Fall in love! If not someday the world becomes to its endWhile you have not yet recognized the telos of life.*

The very nature of philosophical and mystical thinking is multidimensional and it seeks a vision that pushes us forward to set the limits to the use of speculative reason, so that a 'self' on its course of development significantly learns about the misuse and abuse of types of reasoning, and knows specifically that the domain of speculative reason's activities is limited and its boundaries are toughly inviolable. Rumi has alluded to this point in some verses.

1-Speculative reason has its focus on the desired object and to develop workable means to reach that goal or objective; it has nothing to object to the value of its desired object and identified means employed to reach it! Thus, it promotes individualism in a given society, where personally selected goals get chief importance and attention while thoughts and feelings of others are overruled who might receive a critical impact on their lives by enacting upon these goals. Resistance is but natural outcome of such logic and while facing resistance, people perceive people as barriers, their potential enemies and try to get them away by using force. Tyranny operates; the society is fragmented and paves its way towards destruction rather than development (editor).

Nevertheless, the magnificence of **Rumi**'s thought and his fervent emotions should not dazzle us in a way that we turn to accept his thoughts as final words or the absolute truth about the topic. As **Aristotle** once said:

> *I love Plato. However, I have also great passion for Truth. If I were to choose between them, I would certainly align myself with Truth.*

Though Rumi triggers an unremitting challenge to extollers of speculative reason, at certain places he might have taken more positive and constructive stance on speculative reason in his verses, where he was able to establish inadequacy and inefficiency of such reasoning style in explaining human relationship to world around, the God and the universe, he may have well prescribed the potential of its better use instead of completely sinking in pessimism and exhibiting complete loss of hope in speculative reason as he says:

> *If you are to pace the path, you would abandon reason right away!*
>
> *Then you will be given an eye with which you could make your way to the Invisible.*

Using Speculative Reason in Intelligible Life

In "Intelligible Life" we don't regard the speculative reason as troublesome; rather we completely endorse the necessity of its existence and underlying significance of its certain activities in "Intelligible Life". We as human beings are bounded in certain mental and cosmic relationships in life. Speculative reason helps us to determine the nature and scope of such relationships as well as helps us to adjust with these relationships. As mentioned before, a developed mind should accept the reality that expecting sublime truths being uttered from speculative reason is as unnatural as expecting "hearing" from our eyes or using our ears to see.

Therefore, our meaning of intelligible in "Intelligible Life" is not limited to understanding via speculative reason. Although the use of this style of reasoning is permissible in "Intelligible Life" it has limited scope in its use. "Intelligible Life" does not completely disregard what is "is" and that "is" is "necessary", however, it introduces both "what is" and "what ought to be" into human life. In "Intelligible Life" we seek better coordination and balance between speculative reason and practical reason, so that the both might work hand in hand to fulfill all requirements of a developing self.[1] The harmony thus achieved between speculative and practical reasons, reflects itself in a conscience that is conscious of all material and spiritual aspects of human being: *Nay! Man is the evidence of himself*,[2] could be seen as first step toward being a manifestation of "The Reason of Universe" or "Universal Reason" in terms of mystics and spiritual theosophists. Thus, it is for sure that intelligible in "Intelligible Life" has no affinity whatsoever with rationalism as perceived in Western cultures.

1-This cooperation is only possible when these two are in complete harmony. Perhaps Rumi means the reason in harmony with a conscious and active conscience when he speaks of the magnificence of the reason:

> *Do not make sensuality thy vizier, else thy pure spirit will cease from prayer,*
>
> *For this sensuality is full of greed and sees (only) the immediate present, (whereas) the intellect takes thought for the Day of Judgment.* (book IV: 1259-1260)

Greed runs in vain towards the mirage, (though) reason says, "look carefully: it is not water." (book V: 2058)

2-Al-Qyamah: 14.

To explain the difference between "Intelligible Life" and rationalism, we proceed the discussion follows hereafter.

Intelligible Life and Rationalism

One may use Rationalism [as a philosophical term, which is in turn] of two kinds or as a general term to express the state of following the reason:

Rationalism as a philosophical term:

I) Studying individual human nature in particular and its desires in relation to the Nature and fellow men and unearthing the ruling laws of these desires by reason [alone], without any recourse to the understanding and knowledge of spiritual institutions and perfectionist tradition of morality such as study of Psychology. According to intelligible life, this kind of rationalism pursues the knowledge pertaining to fundamental elements of human nature and its adjustment with its natural environment devoid of any study of necessary values or essential morality.

II) Rationalism at both individual and societal levels may imply life governing principles knitted around the chain of universal moral values and rules of pure reason. Though many efforts have been made by some thinkers to prove the possibility of grounding a life style on purely rational principles and rules; consequently, it has resulted in some useful ideas in this field, but all of these thinkers have neglected the inherent conflict in the issue: nonetheless, some of activities of speculative reason demands perfection amounting to mathematical certainty; but it would never undertake the responsibility to steer the man towards "what he wishes for". It is not the Philosophy but it is human heart that quotes: what he wishes for and for which goal he desires and whether these desires are to his best interest or not?

Moreover, keeping into consideration perpetual changes in human existence, it is impossible to devise a universal chain of reality-based rational principles and rules to ensure such stability that would bear every kind of change and alteration. Furthermore, speculative reason severely exposes us to problems, while it doesn't see itself responsible for providing any answer at all. Speculative reason has always readymade interpretations of reality available, but as soon as it confronts more problems related to analysis and synthesis, it fails to provide solid ground to found our arguments over it.

> *Reason is keen-headed but so shaky in her feetSince the soul has been dilapidated and the body has been built on the rubble.*

For example, when we ask the speculative reason: why do we enjoy watching a beautiful landscape? Why the picture showing magnificent colorful trees and a moonlit river is delightful, the reason replies.

This is the description of a beautiful landscape providedby "me" - the reason itself. But the problem is this: what is beauty? And why do we enjoy the landscape in such a mental state? Because its forms and colors correspond with our mental contents, reason replies. Then, we have another question to ask: how should we describe the correspondence between a given landscape and our mental states? In this case speculative reason has no longer a stable stance and replies in a wobbly voice: it might be a matter of association of ideas. That is to say, the blueness of that landscape reminds us that the sky is blue.

Now how should we answer the following question: whether the sporadic relationship between blue petunia and the color of sky is objective or subjective? If this relation is subjective, then it does imply that the beauty of petunia has its roots in human minds, and in general, human mind is the source of all beauties. But if this relation is objective, why does human conception of beauties change with any slight change in his mental states and why people have different tastes and standards for beauty? Why does the same beauty appear differently to different people?

It is for sure that the beauty of an artistic painting is more meaningful for a skillful painter than a peasant or fishermen who have never seen anything but natural landscapes. Should we look for the beauty inside human beings? And to say:

> *What a bride in the soul the picture of her face has decorated*
> *the universe like brides' hands.*[1]

And consequently, should we accept that objective beauties reflect our mental states? Or all appearances of beauty in the universe are objective and our conceptions of beauty are reflections of them? Speculative reason prefers to become agnostic in this case and expresses itself on such issues in poetic language as it does so in the following quatrain that is allegedly of **Khayyam**:

> *Those who mastered themselves in virtues and knowledgeand*
> *so did they become a distinguished man among their*
> *companies.*
>
> *Couldn't make their way out of this dark nightthey just told*
> *a fairytale and passed away.*

Needless to say, not only this quatrain is to exonerate the speculative reason, rather like a prayer that is always read at the end of a religious ceremony, it is always read in the deadlock of questions for a safe exit. For instance, if you challenge speculative reason that someday a tribunal held by intellectuals

---

1-Love Pomes of Rumi.

is going to interrogate you and they may ask you: who has vested in you the absolute authority to determine human intellectual destiny? How will speculative reason confront this question? If it says: I have granted myself this right, their reply would be: haven't you yourself have persistently told us that repeating a claim is not an authentic proof in your favor? If it says: "the tribunal is unjust, how you are even allowed to try me; my achievements throughout the history of mankind are evident for itself; they are the proof". This claim may even face the same fate; the objection can be overruled in minutes by taking a quick snapshot of the history of ideas, since we all know that none of the founders of conflicting schools of thought and ideologies rely on their own feelings and emotions, but their arguments are all attributed to the reason. Thus, this trial is completely just. Now it is reason's turn to answer. Reason will say: deny me, if you could, but it doesn't say that: I am a necessary force in moving toward intellectual evolution, and it could never say that "I am the only force" needed to enter human "Intelligible Life". If you ask the reason about the rest of forces it will surely reiterate Khayyam's quatrain.

If we look at modern societies around us, they have worked out some rules and laws that ensure satisfaction of living a natural life in granted social settings. I do not intend to undermine the value of such satisfaction but I want to question whether satisfaction in social life is only possible path toward human happiness? Speculative reason has a tendency to look at 'Zahir' only and this tendency is dominated in every approach that it advocates for a commendable living [social only, it may appear to others]. Therefore, speculative reason would recommend: a set of rules should be provided that would be most befitting to get things in order in a given social environment. Well, do we have the right to ask: why do we want to conserve the prevailing social environment? What if it is abounded by certain social ills? What if people need personal transformation to reach a better social order? What is the reason of prevalence of given conditions in a society? Why people are forced to take the prescribed regime? Why people cannot take some other course of action? After a long chain of questions, an answer is given [which is itself in the form of a question]: whether majority of people in that society who have already get used to given conditions want a change? Can you lead a change within yourself? It is needless to say that if you can't lead toward a desired change, you will have to follow the prescribed regime. How many people can truly analyze so many 'ifs' and 'buts' and 'whys' and 'why nots'? That is to say, we could not get the answer but in the form of another question and the other party has resolved to keep everyone engaged in the debate, simply because it has no right answer for the posed questions. Do answers of such questions are assured by someone else? I agree:

> *Yes, those who mastered themselves in virtues and knowledge...!!!*

Rationalism has unfortunately the capacity to envisage rules and commandments to put social life in order and that too by imposing certain labels and restrictions over the exaggerated animosity at its best. For the time being the manifesto for peaceful co-existence seems magnificent to comply with. But under-currents of unseasoned "natural selves" keep the volcano active and ready to erupt at the most unfortunate moments in the history. No amount of restrictions, rational laws or social sanctions can prevent the natural disaster from following. It is manifested with full grandeur leading to complete disruption of society in which only natural style of living was recognized as most suitable. The natural consequences are now infested with self revolts in the form of wars and famines which pave the ground for wild contests and so the magnificent palace of laws falls   down   as   the   volcano   explodes   bursting everythingnaturally into raging flames and everything reduced to nothingness except few archives to live in the celebrated history of human kind.[1]Against such extremism, rationalism took the lead to sanction authority to secular reason to pursue knowledge in a valueless framework. We could see such extremist reactions in classic and modern psychology, as a psychologist says:

> Classic psychology was "the bodiless head" and modern psychology is "the headless body".

This weakness of rationalism represents the inadequacy of pure rationalism in social life only, and thus, it does not disqualify it thoroughly. To state the matter more clearly, no doubt, rationalism in social life is an essential factor, but human life, in its individual existence, cannot be fully realized in a holistic fashion by relying completely on the guidelines provided by the speculative reason; therefore, we recommend developing great passion to experience development in other aspects of life as well.

Life lived in pursuit of pure rationalism could be seen as a reaction to Medieval Western theocracy that was to sanction divine abstractive authority to specific human societies by devaluing moderate sensuality in some and valuing and pure consciences of others promoting sectarianism. Such sense of holy powers not only insinuated [holy wars in world communities but they also dealt with their internal rebels with

---

1-About feelings of togetherness in American culture Bogosian wrote in his book titled, Sex, drugs and rock and Roll: As a nation we sit at a huge rock concert singing along to some well-known anthem of cloying sentiment. We love the feeling, the togetherness, the righteousness of the cause. As we watch the evening news or read the daily tabloids, we are shocked together, we are pleased together, we are entertained together, we are saddened together. Unfortunately, when the concert is over, we get back in our cars, drive home, and go to bed. It is only rock and roll. (Bogosian, Eric, Sex, Drugs, and Rock and Roll, Harper, Collins, N.Y. N.Y. 1950, p. xvi.) (editor).

an iron hand, e.g. witch hunt and so called Puritan movement in North America].

Managing reconciliation between theocracy and rationalism had been very hard. Some thinkers like Nietzsche and Hegel have tried to deify man. They have blatantly tried to seek human glory in human acts of bravery, chivalry, benevolence and forgiveness as were the hallmarks of Muslim Philosophy and theosophy. They also tried to craft a model of divine man and proposed this model as propeller of humanity and safe deliverance of humankind away from barbaric shores of animalism. It became a popular paradigm to work on to build future. We could call this eclectic school "rationalist-humanism".

Whether or not this synthesis has been able to command truth? Needless to say, this synthesis itself stands as yet 'another school' added without being able to achieve reconciliation between the previously discussed two schools. Rationalism defends itself strongly against anything which has to do with the sacred and the sacrilege. It was too egotist for such people to bear with the egoism of the common, that simple and common could be deified; their ideas, words and deeds could be seen as manifestations of the Divinity and Truth. Wasn't it so that the weaklings, the commoners were responsible for all wrong deeds - bloodshed, injustice and violence?

The only way, thus, is to reconcile these schools with each other in its true sense; both of these should accept that until human egoism is seasoned by moving into "Intelligible Life", in other words, until and unless it leaves the station of "the natural life" it would not be able to move forward in the "human history". Both schools will remain stuck in course of evolution and would be unable to reach their predestined goals. The process of moving from "egoistic naturalism" into "Intelligible

Life" unveils positive elements of both schools and harmonizes them with the reality of human existence. The positive elements are:

I) Paying serious attention to rational aspect of human nature and celebrating the idea that the every individual is such a being of reason and conscience, which is if cultivated with humanistic – and not mechanistic or deterministic – sound instructions, everyone will have better chance to accept the role of divinity in life and by doing so they will play their practical roles more effectively both in individual and social life. Since a sound human reason and conscience could well understand the harmful effects of being plunged in "natural life", especially through reading dark lines of history of naturalism, and try to revise it. No one could evaluate "reason" and "good conscience" like these two trustworthy divine agents [theocracy and rationalism]. These trustworthy harbingers could envision themselves as tools for organizing and crafting practical frameworks of those realities and truths that are bestowed to them for mastery. Unless we get this divine sanction, the reason and good conscience, two purely natural human processes, will remain devoid of handy tools and a work plan to achieve "Intelligible Life".

That is to say, they will be able to bring people out of the strong spell of animalistic egotism, reincarnating them into individuals who are charged with dynamism of "Intelligible Life". They will transform from a brute selfish animal into a highly engaged moral person. These two forces, human reason and conscience will be evident enough to claim another human urgent need for theosophy.

II) The influence of absolute Divine authority in human affairs, but not in such an abstract form that will deprive human beings from sensing, moral judgment and purity of conscience to work constructively for building social values and ethos of a Muslim culture, for such activities   are manifestations in themselves of divine authority in human affairs.

In one of verses related to "Intelligible Life", we read: "... **and he who would live might live by clear proof**"[1] Needless to say, this clear proof is provided by good moral judgment and pure consciences. That is why in Islam divine authority has three appearances:

I. Those revealed principles, laws and obligations that Holy Prophet Muhammad (SAW) conveyed to humanity.

II. Better human sensing and pure consciences that interpret and master them to perfection.

III. Individual human reasons and consciences that followed the practices of masters.

In both of first and second appearances, the principle of consultation reveals that divine element doesn't ground itself through devaluing human reason and conscience, but it is the other way round, these two trustworthy agents divinizes human self by realizing the manifesto of "Intelligible Life".

1- Al-Anfal: 42.

Chapter Three

Dimensions of Intelligible Life

This chapter examines in detail various factors constituting the definition of intelligible life and their possible impact upon human social life. The author asserts here that this life style can bring desired change in human life if people agree to undergo eleven transformations. The chapter is divided into following sections:

1. Factors constituting definition of intelligible life
   - ✓ *Developing Consciousness*
   - ✓ *Creating a personal Will.*
   - ✓ *Reconstructing the Personality*
   - ✓ *Knowing the Ultimate Telos of Life*
   - ✓ *Following the Course of Intellectual Evolution*

2. Human Potential for Intelligible Life
   - ✓ *Eleven-fold transformations*

3. True Scope of Intelligible Life

4. Influence of Intelligible Life on Human Social Living
   - ✓ *Teleological dimension*
   - ✓ *Instrumental dimension*

Previously proposed definition of intelligible life constitutes several important factors. To expound theses components we must study individual factors in detail:

1) **Developing Consciousness:** being conscious of the fact that "I am alive" is other than unconsciously being moved into the stream of life like other animals. Unconscious participation in the stream of life is a desirable state for lowly creatures and they move toward it by their instinctive nature which stays away from the undesirable.

This autonomous orientation of 'staying away from the undesirable' is an essential characteristic of human natural life-style as well, which is a delicate product of countless interactions of its inherent characteristics with the natural environment. This delicate product (human being) which continues its movement with seven million "whys"[1], without being conscious of its inherent nature, its qualifying constituents and without being aware of what could be constructed with this inherent nature or constituent qualities is a dependent phenomenon that has no hope to be counted as an independent reality. Indeed, all aspects and activities of human life that are involved in living such an unconscious life are caused by factors that are outside him and sometimes they remain invisible because of their apparent missing connection with human self. Whenever this man begins his propositions with "I", this just implies that his propositions are all about an external factor. For example, if he says: "I think" it implies that "They think" or "I smile" does imply that "He/she smiles" or "I am crying" does imply that "He/she is crying" and so on.

It is only the consciousness of independent life [*Lebenbewusstsein*] that interprets principles and values for

---

1- It is only through such evolutionist conception of life that we could not only understand what happens in the body of living beings, rather we will be able to answer seven millions "whys" about the nature of life, **AlexanderOparin**, Russian biologist, once said (*Life: its nature and source of evolution*: 83[translated into Persian by **Hashem Banitarfi**]). It is indeed seven million and one "whys" with the why that addresses the theory of evolution itself.

human self enabling it to distinguish "I" from "He/she" and "I" from "That". The fact that history has always allowed more room for 'the natural' in comparison to the human, it is due to this very unconsciousness of life's principles and values. Moreover, human history has always been subjugated by unconscious forces and with growing time these blind forces have become more and more powerful, making the history of human slavery more colorful.

> *Since consciousness is the inmost nature and essence of the soul,The more aware one is the more spiritual one is.*
>
> *Awareness is the effect of the spirit: anyone who has this in excess is a man of God.*
>
> *Since there are consciousnesses beyond this (bodily) nature, in that (spiritual) arena these (sensual) souls are (like) inanimate matter.*
>
> *The first soul is the theatre of the (Divine) court; The Soul of the soul is verily the theatre of God (Himself).*[1]

We will summarize these verses in the succinct word of consciousness and its role in "Intelligible Life". Soul is self-consciousness.[2]Therefore, nobody could claim for having intelligible life, but those who are already conscious of the identity, principles and values of their life. This shows clearly why Islam strongly insists on acquiring self-consciousness! For this reason, in Islam, the path leading to our ultimate destination is "Intelligible Life" and this intelligible life would never be realized without growing in consciousness:

1- Mathnavi' Ma'navi, book VI: 149-152.

2- "Jan" in Persian carries a meaning for which I believe we have no equivalent in English but in German we have two words, Geist/Seele, that are used in similar way that we use Ruh / Jan in Persian. (Translator)

What is religion? Taking oneself off the earthMay thus pure
soul to become conscious of itself?[1]

It is for sure that this consciousness is an outcome of intellectual efforts to know the identity, principles and values of human life. This aspect of our definition of "Intelligible Life", viz. the necessity of consciousness of "life as it is" and "life as it ought to be", is underlined in following verse of Holy Quran:

…that he who would perish might perish by clear proof, and
he who would live might live by clear proof…[2]

According to this holy word, a man who is not able to become conscious of life and to demonstrate the eligibility of every stage of his life through clear proofs, his life is not "Intelligible", but it is an unconscious phenomenon sustained under the spell of natural laws and blind forces.

2) Creating a Personal Will. Second aspect of "Intelligible Life" is organizing one's physical life taking care of the deterministic and semi-deterministic forces in operation by developing one's free will and training it to execute itself in natural realization of all evolutionary goals particularly regarding to attainment of intellectual consciousness in life.

To understand this factor and its importance in "Intelligible Life", we need to settle some issues regarding it. They are discussed below:

First issue: the most vital role that consciousness plays in life is that it helps people to rein certain deterministic forces by developing subtle understanding of natural laws and principles that govern these forces. Through such knowledge persons are able to explore the scope of their true freedom while fulfilling

---

1- From the verses of Dr. Muhammad Iqbal known in Iran as Iqbal e Lahori.
2- Al-Anfal: 42.

all other physical and social necessities of life. This issue is of deep concern to people who really crave for an "Intelligible Life" and it should be clear that without developing such awareness, and without practicing upon principles learned through the awareness, laying any claim of entering into intelligible life will be nothing more than a hyperbole. It is but the truth.

The significance of this issue has reminded me of a verse from **Imam Hussein**'s prayer, he was reciting in the desert of Arafat:

> *O' my God! Make me conscious of the necessities of my existence.*

Indeed this verse that characterizes the serious relationship between human soul and the Sublime Perfection.

On a closer look, we encounter another delicate reality, i.e. escape vs. trap of necessities of life. It is dawned that sensing complete freedom in denying all personal and social necessities is as harmful as sensing oneself as entrapped in necessities of life, since in both cases we misconceive the reality. The secret lies in working out a careful balance which quotes true freedom for the wayfarers who pace the path of intelligible life. Therefore, one must learn to discard the fear from the very beginning that we have no liberty whatsoever in the world of natural laws and forces. In the same spirit, one should never deceive oneself with the super-ambitious hope that humans enjoy absolute liberty. Our liberty in the world of natural laws is like narrow veins of diamond spread in a thick piece of coal, existing independently in their full brightness in darkness of a thick piece of coal.

The determinism makes people compulsive in their habits; they lovingly participate in the quixotic battle against natural laws and forces in hope to win. When people have such a grandiose image attached with their compulsory habits, it becomes hard to tell anyone not to be a hard core determinist. All we can do is to undertake a messianic enterprise to help them disentangle from the chain of blind slavery of *"Isness"* or "narcissism". The gradual awareness of rational self and discovering inner potential will break bonds of the captivity, and the immanent joy of getting released will keep enhancing sense of freedom. It will help people gradually transform their ordinary lives into "intelligible" ones or at least we would be able to persuade them to come into the sphere, may be just inside the borderline. This proposal is not an end to the controversial debate on the dilemma of necessity and liberty in humanities, but it is just an effort to show the possibility and simplicity of introducing people into "Intelligible Life".

We believe that putting an end to all scientific pursuits and exploration in search of solutions to countless chronic problems humans and humanity are suffering would be an unforgivable injustice to science and human beings. The scope of this adventure has been as huge in length, width, depth in any temporal context as humanity itself. But we cannot wait forever and keep postponing the vital project of "Intelligible Life" for science to come for its everlasting solution. How can we be so sure of the fact that one day an anthropologist or sociologist would arise with a theory solving eternal dilemma of necessity and freedom for good. Undoubtedly, I have the same appetite for "Intelligible Life" as any other person one thousand or ten thousand years later than me will be.

The critical point in this discussion celebrates the fact fundamental factors of "Intelligible Life" have been determined through a logical vision based on realities which are not inconsistent with findings of say volumes of scientific research done in past 500 years to solve necessity/freedom dilemma. Today like other times before, we can rely on this realist logic that every man who is conscious of his present and future situations and feels himself powerful enough to move himself from the situation that is an effect of despicable corporeal aims and incentives, must strive at his best to be moved to the next situation in the hierarchy. If he is hyper-sensitive about "freedom", he could title this divine movement as "absolute necessity", but he must make this effort and take that step and try to wipe himself out of any blind sensitivity whether of "freedom" or of "necessity". But we all know that these words are merely contractual forms for communicating personal ideas lacking in independent objectivity.

For example, anyone who feels himself capable enough to move himself from a situation surrounded by evil ambitions to a higher state enthused by divine human concerns and philanthropic values, taking that step becomes an "absolute necessity". Have you ever heard the story of man's confrontation with necessity/freedom dilemma? Two schools of thought narrate this story:

I. Those who believe that the Mother Nature is the mover of the cradle, and 'necessarily'all humans are in the cradle, and step out only once and forever at the time when the earth has opened her mouth to swallow him. To state the matter more clearly, one departs this cradle only to enter one's grave.

II. Those who say that human dwelling in natural cradle of necessity is only the peculiarity of its infancy and after leaving this stage of life man is free move anywhere. The negligence of this school is exactly opposite of the first, breeding another kind of extremism. Alas! Both of these attitudes play the same promising role in veiling truth from mankind.

Second issue: Realization of the path of freedom moving towards liberty. "Intelligible Life" begins from emancipation and after passing through the stage of freedom for further development and final finished product is achieved in the lofty stage of liberty. Scholars do not usually distinguish between these three stages of "emancipation", "freedom" and "liberty", which is a must for complete understanding of the process.

Emancipation:deliverance from all bondages that block human beings on their road to development, whether these bondages are physical or psychological, obligatory or contractual. For instance, a person kept captive in a room, when released takes a sigh of relief, his physical captivity was the major concern for him. Similarly, another person, who owes somebody something like debt, feels released from the obligation on full payment. Similar feelings are observed on release from mental tensions and anxieties.

Freedom:apart from being released from bondages a person is free to choose his own way to act regardless of the point whether the way chosen by him is good or bad, magnificent or despicable, ugly or beautiful. Here, the individuals have better sense of independence and upholding selfhood than in the stage of emancipation, but it cannot be estimated whether the freedom earned will realize best of objectives. There is always a chance that the glorious freedom attained might be spoiled by unrestrained behaviors or will be ruined by poor choice.

Liberty: comprehensive knowledge of the self of both positive and negative outcomes of a choice and using freedom to reach goodness and development and avoiding loss and failure. If we see freedom as the reason, then liberty entails acquiring rationalism through rational activity. In the same way, if we see freedom as physical light, then liberty is involving in the necessary or useful task which is done in that light.

Human life is like crystal clear soft water that flows out of a source, but freedom flows out of human life like limpid and life-giving water. To be benefited from this water more effectively, we need a gardener to cultivate trees, flowers and farm lands by watering them at right time in right amount. Liberty is using freedom by the self for personal development to cultivate human dignity. The more flexible and facilitative a society is to allow personal developments of individuals by using freedom to acquire liberty, the more it will be benefited from "Intelligible Life". This factor of our definition is derived from the following verse:

... strive with one another to hasten to virtuous deeds....[1]

There is no room for any doubt that "competition" and "virtuous deeds" both imply arbitrary efforts, since the objectives that we seek by necessity could be described as "good" only if they have been achieved by human freedom; because whenever "good" and "evil" are attributed to human actions they are generated from the normative concepts and their attribution to corresponding human actions is wholly contingent upon the role that human liberty plays in enacting them. "The Righteous" is someone who never involves himself in evil doings while having the possibility to do so. "The Evil" is someone who has a strong tendency to involve himself in evil doings while having the possibility to act righteously and wisely.

Third issue: the influence of social environment and other authorities in the society in facilitating pedagogues of the intelligible life through making goodness and values more accessible to human beings. As we had mentioned previously, liberty is like limpid life-giving water which flows out of human life and seeks goodness, development and perfection by its nature. This latter quality does not flourish in vacuum but in an environment that has already been prepared by the authorities and pedagogues for the said purpose. An uncongenial environment washes out the possibility for human

---

1- Al-Ma'eda: 48. The necessity of competing for reaching to goodness and perfection has also been indicated in other verses such as Al-Baqara: 149.

liberty to be flourished. Unless authorities and pedagogues of a society won't be able to make their people conscious of the magnificence of human values, their people will undoubtedly waste their precious freedom. If we liken freedom to regular movement of the stones of a mill, of course, to initiate movement of mill an external force is needed, and if free activities of life have their roots in life itself, then environment and the ideas of authorities and pedagogues of the society are the grains which are poured into the mill. The mill will change those grains into wheat and thus the food supply for the society will be rest assured.

This is a mill that never stops working. If there are no materials available externally to be poured in for grinding, it may start processing its internal contents, for instance its temptations and futile idea, and keep the supply to society continued with lowly ideas of greed and selfishness; it isn't far from impossible that the mill would start to grind itself very soon and shatter itself, since once started, it cannot stop its autonomous working.

Another alternative is still possible that the authorities of the mill may choose to grind ordinary people entrapped in worldly life and enjoy taking advantage of their personal freedom. If they will ever wake up from their wild fantasy into reality they would be murmuring the following verse of **Lermantov:**

> *We touch the bowl of life with our lips while we have already shut our tearful eyes, but the day comes that death opens our eyes and gets whatever we once loved in our life, only on that day we will find it out that our bowl was empty from the*

start, and we have not drunk but imaginary wine from this bowl.[1]

If mill of human freedom works in a logical manner and processes only "Intelligible" materials and thence get its soul intelligiblized, that soul would never whine:

The world is like a bubble/ but what a bubble / not on the water/ but on a mirage/ a dreamy mirage which occurs in a habitual drunkard's sleep.[2]

3) Re-constructing the Personality:[3]There is no doubt that it is the ideal of all civilized nations to be constructed in their desired form. The inspiration and ideal of "becoming" have not emerged in the same form in different societies in different periods of time. This inspiration comes directly from how an ideal has been defined as desirable for an individual or a society in a given time.

It is noteworthy indeed that if something is to be introduced into a society in the form of an ideal, it should be seen as the very truth that the people of that society have always been seriously looking for in order to shape themselves according to. Since most of the civilizations have always dared to introduce such truths as desired ideals into societies that were keenly desirable for the authorities (such as truths of Papal theocracy in medieval age), we are unable to witness authentic human qualities, capacities and desires emerging in their truest and perfect representation in due course of history. It gives us point

---

1- World's Most Beautiful Masterpieces: 293.

2-This quatrain is allegedly of Khayyam.

3- Personality is the external and not internal dimension of ourselves; we need to distinguish clearly that personality is the outer cover, the traits and behaviors through which others know us and the self is our intrinsic dimension -how do we view us and what do we know about our characteristics, weaknesses and strengths that constitute us (editor).

to ponder, what we are really expecting from human evolution, when the scientists have agreed that biological or physiological evolution in human beings have stopped (if we take fixed number of chromosomes as means of identification of species); the evolution now is largely challenged at fronts of mental, social or psychological aspects of human life.[1] However, considering threefold human existence, physical, psychological and social, the human relationship with nature and natural laws has also not much changed in essence but only the sublime differences lie in the degrees of environmental qualities and the simplicity and/or complexity of human relationship with other human beings and with nature, and last but not the least the quality and the scope of such relationships.

Today it is evident that no society has been yet completely successful in realizing all of human authentic qualities, capacities and desires to inscribe this fabulous achievement in its history. One of the authentic human qualities much celebrated throughout the human history is 'good living', rendered as the most potent agent for realizing positive potential leading to true happiness. This ideal quality in human beings could not be denied but through fallacies. In order to establish this reality we need to know which life style really offers this quality? Though the obvious choice would be "Intelligible Life", still we would like to make it clear for our audience how does intelligible life enables us to realize this ideal of "good living".

It has already been much argued by us that human selfhood in its course of becoming enjoys the intelligible life style, since the "Intelligibility" of life is a constant motivation in itself that

---

1- See e.g. Consilience by E. O. Wilson or editor's commentary over it: The Future of Knowledge Theory (editor).

pushes life forward. We hear the following words resounding as they become gradually an intelligible reality:

How accursed is he whose yesterday is better than his today and how short of change is the one whose two days are the same![1]

Take the new and surrender the old, for every "this year" of thine is superior to three "previous years".[2]

* * *

Baghdad is the same you have already seen and heard of/ go after a new beloved, why are you so fond of cured meat? / If you have already tried the cauldron of the universe/ it has the same taste yet you don't need to try it again.[3]

* * *

Revive your faith, but not just with your tongue, secretly to your lusts why have you clung? / When lusts are fresh, faith can't be any more, Lust is the very key that locks the door![4]

Needless to say, "moving forward" in this sense doesn't imply transgressing the boundaries of abstract time and pure space; rather it refers to the transformation of naïve and elementary emotions into sublime ones and in turn the transformation of particular reasoning into more universal reasoning. These transformations pave the way for the ascent of free will into the stage of liberty.

1-There is a statement in Nahj-ol-balaghe uttered in the same spirit by Imam Ali (p.b.u.h).

2-Mathnavi' Ma'navi, book V: 809.

3-Love Poems of Rumi.

4-Mathnavi' Ma'navi, bookI: 1086-1087.

The ultimate unity of human self will not be possible without these threefold transformations. The naïve and elementary emotions are nothing but temporary affections. The more the influence of these affections (which are merely passive in their nature) gets increased, the lesser will be the opportunity for human self to be developed. "Intelligible Life" does not deny human affections in general, but it simply asks to harness these affectations and immature infatuations by observing selfhood.[1]

Thus, with growing selfhood the affectation of sensual and baseless pleasures will be changed into a sensible taste (zawq) which originates from reasoning and liberty. Noting will remain acceptable which is affected by a self-centered egotism as persons will learn to reflect over their own thoughts and actions. They will be able to realize the inappropriateness in their mannerism soon and will be able to rebuild their relationships in life. It is not just the self-esteem which is a desired quality of selfhood but it is the purified self-respect and self-esteem, free from shades of narcissism and egotism, which harbingers lofty ideals in commanding principles of human life. In the absence of such rationalized purity there will be no loftiness and all ideals will remain merely escalated affections, the dreams which cannot be envisioned to reality promoting a sense of loss than happiness. The most explicative instances of "naïve" and "escalated" affections would be found in the sphere of sorrows which are of two kinds:

I. Ordinary sorrows which occur as a result of the dissatisfaction of worldly desires and instinctual pleasures.

II. The loftiest sorrows that are more valuable than any pleasure whatsoever:

1- Selfhood here is understood in Iqbalian terms which means rational construction of one's thought and personality according to Divine standards of morality. (editor)

If you don't make your heart her home,

Howcould you be so lighthearted?

If you don't choose her sorrow,

Whichsorrow would you deserve to choose?[1]

The latter sorrow is not a personal loss but unifying with the feeling of human loss at large; resulting passion has created so many brilliant figures in human history – the artists, poets and philanthropists. Though many people find it residing in the lonely corners of their hearts and soul, but they deem it their personal possession, finding hard to express it thoroughly, whereas few others fathom its magnificence and value and not only learn to communicate through it, their mastery generates an everlasting piece of art, [like Mona Lisa[2] or like Taj Mahal of Agra][3]. This holy boon manifests itself in a very lofty escalated affection inside one's self, when rationality, freedom and liberty are elevated to the degree that exceeds human bounds to enter divine sphere, hinting at the real scope of human intellectual evolution.

When human personality starts shaping itself by reconstruction, pure and abstract reasoning becomes saturated of such lofty and escalated affections; this affect is more wholesome and qualitative in nature than "2 plus 2 equals 4" kind of quantification, easily being declared as a natural activity of adding up more neural networks in brain. When this evolution (evolution in affections and reasoning) occurs, human bondages, whether natural or environmental, social or relational, or the bondages based on animal lusts, all are

---

1- Feyze Kashani.

2-Famous painting of Leonardo Da Vinci.

3- The mausoleum of 5th Moghal emperor Shah Jahan and his Queen Mumtaz Mahal located in Agra, India.

transformed into freedom and liberty. It is through this threefold transformations that human personality enters into its course of evolution. This personal transformation is the most fundamental aspect of "Intelligible Life" without achieving it any individual or society has no right to claim any evolution or being on path of "Intelligible Life"; the sphere of this enlightened intelligible life is not an isolated community but it is quite delightfully submerged in main stream of the life and the living.

During the course of its becoming, human personality takes advantage of both "internal" and "external" realities, i.e., inner enthusiasm for perfection and strengthening of capacities that realize this enthusiasm on one hand, and on the other preparing the outside world for this actualized potential under the guidance of sympathetic pedagogues with humanist orientation. These are the founding principal for reconstruction of human personality and only a little negligence in their use may change persons for the worst, for instance, they may become the tools of dehumanization in society.

The following verses of Holy Quran remind the significance of this factor:

> **1-** *Whoever does good whether male or female and he/she is a believer, we will most certainly make him/her live a happy (pure) life [which is the very same "Intelligible Life"].*[1]

There is no doubt that ordinary worldly life – which knows no ideal but carnal lusts and earthly pleasures – is not "Pure Life" in Quranic terms. The purity of life has its origin in the actualization of true nature of life in human existence encompassing it fully and broadening its influence in all of its aspects. There is no room for any doubt that the most

---

1-Al-Nahl: 97.

fundamental aspect of true nature of life is "evolutionary becoming", that God has given to all human beings.

2- Allah confirms those who believe with the sure word in this world's life and in the hereafter.[1]

We know that living on the basis of subsistent rational principles and laws which lay the unifying ground for human personality in the course of systematic evolution in life, is a characteristic of "Intelligible Life", and not of "Natural Life", since the latter is restricted to physical interactions with people and environment. Any natural occurrence in human life is an effect of factors which are all outside the control of human self, therefore, it is illogical to attribute such occurrences to human personality that has no authority whatsoever in this domain. Therefore, "Sure Word" in above mentioned verse refers to understanding of rational principles and laws that lays the foundation for unity of ever-evolving human selfhood.

How to construct/ reconstruct personality?

Human personality is constructible and could be gradually constructed through rational and intuitive calculations of evolutionary ideals. This is a self-evident and indisputable truth for every anthropologist. The problem lies in how should we construct human personality? Is the course of construction so unbearable that nobody could venture to pace on? No, it not the case, because we know, "the best reason for the possibility of a thing is the occurrence of the same thing". When you see a full-blown tree somewhere it would seem nonsense to ask if a tree could grow here or not. Because there is no other conceivable reason more evident, sensible and decisive than the tree that has already grown there.

1-Ibrahim: 27.

In our case, human history has revealed the most evident, sensible and decisive reason through the very existence of Abraham's disciples, however they are in minority, but they are the most serious manifestations of humanity. A brief review of the history of "Intelligible Life" will show us the futility of disputations. We must only find the *correct way* of this construction. To begin with, we should know that this latter task is simultaneously so hard and too simple. It is so hard, since we have been absorbed in earthborn lusts of "natural life" insofar as the perception lasts that ascension may deprive us of our "satisfactions" and this feeling is torturous like death as if our soul was going to leave the body. Nevertheless, this construction is also too simple; too simple than we could perceive it, because in order to get into the course of this self-construction we need to develop a little awareness about two facts:

I. Know that human being is different from animal.

II. Learn to develop a will to be a human.

After getting the awareness:

> *Get into the path in silence*
>
> *The path will show you how to pace.*[1]

It is not hard to know who may take charge of constructing and reconstructing personalities, of course everybody knows that the job belongs to teachers and pedagogues, the harder is to submit before them – to die before death as Rumi commands.

Millions of personalities have evolved under the prescribed influence of formal education, media and social environment; there are doves that are changed into vultures and there are vultures that get into the path of becoming a dove. Is there

---

1- A'tar

anyone who is mourning on losing the path of becoming a 'Royal Falcon'?[1]

The question "if human personality could get into the course of construction", therefore, appears more like a joke than a scientific dilemma. What is of greater significance here is to decide through which stations the personality should pass to be constructed? The answer of this question has been the subject matter of all our debates until now reiterating again and again: Pass (evolving) through naïve stages of "natural life" into the mature stages of "Intelligible Life", because it is always the sore grapes that evolve into sweet grapes. Never would any sweet grapes appear all at once from nowhere.

4) Knowing the Ultimate Telos[2]of Life. Having taken into precise consideration the meanings of "Telos" and "The Ultimate Telos of Life", there remains no room for doubt that this teleological goal is not consistent with being swamped with deterministic and semi-deterministic desires of "natural self" –

1- The souls enriched by divine self-knowledge, an allegory that Rumi has used in Mathnavi to signify prophets, saints and Wali of Allah, the concept has been elaborated by John Renard in his All the King's Falcon's: Rumi on Prophets and Revelations.

2-Telos has been understood as the "purpose" or "goal" related to our physical living. The term has been extensively used in the writings of Aristotle in his study of Biology while studying causes of behavior and differentiating between causes of animal and human behaviors. Whereas, Aristotle and Hegel found that survival of humanity is the ultimate Telos and thus, service of life is the individual telos of every individual. However, the view of modern 20th century philosophers is different. Naturalists do not assign any collective purpose or higher aim to life. In modern pragmatism and Utilitarianism, individual physical needs take precedence over the rest. Evolutionary psychologists aiming to seek more affinity between human beings and animals rather than distinguishing between the two do not find huge differences between human and animal behaviors. Causes of everyday behavior are thus seen as grounded in our basic physiological needs, such as hunger, thirst, sleep, and sex. Since, these needs are unavoidable, they are recognized as basic human needs – the most natural ones as our survival of earthly life depends upon the satisfaction of these needs. (editor) that the sense of liberty makes them more pleasant – which not only does not help us to achieve "The Ultimate Telos of Life", rather we can not envisage any ultimate telos of life in the context of natural life at all. Achieving the ultimate goal of life needs two essential prerequisites, without which any debate around this subject will be nothing but an idle talk. These two prerequisites are:

I) Logical application of those common sense activities that are in harmony with pure conscience and human primal self (This point will be discussed in full length in later sections of the topic)

II) Having strong will to take advantages of those rational activities that assist us to touch the epic of the 'Telos'. The Ultimate Telos of Life is, as we have declared previously,the participation in general cosmic movement toward supreme perfection which is the fifth factor of our definition of "Intelligible Life". What does "participating in general cosmic movement" imply? According to a verse of Holy Quran:

> And I have not created the jinn and the men except that they should serve me.[1]

That is to say, participating in general cosmic movement implies setting oneself under the direction of divinity and purifying the spirit from all carnal lusts and moral vices through undertaking those religious obligations that have been prescribed by holy prophets and by constructing one's conscience through undertaking all transcendental imperatives and thus changing "Metaphorical Ego" into "Real Ego"; by doing so all human physical and mental movements and pauses will take the form of "divine service". When a real consciousness of the necessity of participating in general cosmic movement is

---

1-Al-Dhariyat: 57.

associated with a strong will for movement, the result is becoming acquainted with the Ultimate Telos of Life. Finally, this goal is not a limited truth, since divine presence is not limited in itself.

After being acquainted with the Ultimate Telos of Life, all human physical and mental activities take the form of "divine services" at Divine Threshold. Farming is as much of a "divine service" in this sense as is working in a factory may be called a "divine service". Scientific research done in humanities and cosmology will be rendered as "divine service" as well as working in a laboratory will be a "divine service". Finally, being acquainted with this ultimate telos of life involves a significant consequence that is restricted to the following goal.

> *Say, surely my prayer and my sacrifice and my life and my death are (all) for Allah, the lord of the worlds.*[1]

This Quranic verse explains how one could become acquainted with the Ultimate Telos of Life in a very explicit way to the extent that having consciousness of his participation in general cosmic movement the man becomes so fond of God (the Supreme Perfection) that every single instance of his life, whether spiritual or material, is filled with God, and this living consciousness of God justifies the enthusiasm of human spirit for perfection, which otherwise would have never been realized with any other telos.

Coming back to *"And I have not created the jinn and the men except that they should serve me"*, the *"Divine Service"* here implies the very consciousness of participation in the general cosmic movement by establishing voluntary relationship with the God. Moreover, fulfilling all religious obligations fills

---

1-Al-Ana'm: 162.

human spirit with eternal sense of "presence", i.e. being in constant communication withSupreme Perfection.

Despite all positive arguments, the "Telos of Life" remains among one of the most controversial issues, pronounced by natural scientists as "Illusion of the Philosophy",[1] partly because of the sophisticated words almost unintelligible to the common of 21st century, and partly due to massive disputations over the implications of these words, which many people deem unavoidable. Sa'di says, if I cannot fathom it so:

> *It is better to sit and be patientand just to think of my personal affairs.*

5) Following the Course of Intellectual Evolution. We need to deliberate uponthe fact that although science has enough material to give a comprehensive description of the process of evolution regarding physical nature and living things, but when it comes to human beings and begins to describe human intellectual evolution in history, the historians, the social anthropologists always culminate at epics of industrial or technological developments, which have their roots in mental craft of some geniuses. Although we know that unrelenting pursuit of knowledge and hard work has always been the hallmark of such geniuses and will remain the same in future as well, but the question raised here is: whether the discovery or invention is an outcome of individual or group effort of scientists and researchers? Whether it has been made possible by establishing logical connection with preexisting ideas or it was a result of a sudden, spontaneous and sparkling idea in the mind of the inventor, who with his new idea is able to refute the existing knowledge?

1- See Sigmund Freud's Last lecture on Psychoanalysis. (editor)

Neither a sociologist nor a philosopher, however, could demonstrate it through logical and convincing debate that industrial and technological developments marking the intellectual epoch in human history are the products of a logical system of preexisting ideas, generating the paradox: how we are able to claim that the man has achieved any success in his course of intellectual evolution at all. It seems that we humans are always deceived by two misconceptions:

I) Our great enthusiasm for perfection and growth is always mistaken with actual perfection and growth. That is to say, this very enthusiasm misleads us to the belief that we have already achieved real perfection (i.e. we may claim that we are doing better than people did in the past but what about future? Won't they have any chance to perform better than us?).

II) The inability of distinguishing between individual human beings and the humanity at large; we tend to take credit of person's individual work, assuming that being human everybody perhaps share all properties of human beings and thus one has the right to own individual works of persons belonging to their family, community, nation or race. Therefore, when anybody says, I live in the twentieth century; he is trying to say that I am the twentieth century itself with all its appearances!! This miscalculation results in this wonderful conclusion that "So, I have intellectually evolved as well!"[1]

Moreover, "intellectual" and "evolution" may appear to some naïve minds as an odd combination and they may ask us what do you mean by this "intellectual evolution"? Is it possible for the people to understand "intellectual evolution" and to bear

---

1-To understand whether these delusions are right or wrong we must return to previous discussions (chapter one).

the difficulties of leaving earthborn desires of pure natural life and acquiring consciousness to reach so called intelligent evolution? I say: yes he could, if human brain has the capability to understand 2 plus 2 equals 4, "the whole is bigger than parts" and "everything is identical with itself and is nothing but itself", the same brain has the capability to understand doing duties for reaching to real good – which necessitates those duties – and to try to achieve this good with the aid of reason and conscience.

He should also know that doing duties for realizing the real good reinforces the spirit of justice and perseverance in individual, while doing duties for reward and avoiding punishment makes a machine of him that cannot release itself of the bondage of necessity that he has made it himself. That is to say, rewards and punishments, both are churned out to be another deterministic factor. As Rumi says:

> He's fallen in hell's pit now, it's too late
>
> and it's his own fault—it's not down to fate.
>
> He's thrown himself inside such a deep pit
>
> that I can't measure the full depth of it.[1]

We assert that human mind works so brilliantly following natural life style for acquiring wealth, dignity and social reputation and in defeating his rivals. We are curious to know whether or not this mind could reorient its capabilities toward such loftiest ideals as humanitarianism, promoting justice and seeking goodness with a strong will?

1- Mathnavi'Ma'navi: book I, 3833-3834.

Human Potential for Intelligible Life

Does humanity have the necessary potential for "Intelligible Life"? Once an audience in my lectures on intelligible life asked me:

> *Will you be able to carry forty tons of cargo on a hand cart through a bottleneck? Haven't you forgotten about the quote that you gave in your writing about the thinker who was studying the ideals of common men and was soon disheartened after hearing so many absurd and narrow-minded responses? As you may strongly endorse the idea that this later group of people always constitute the majority of every society, don't you take it for granted that those who transcend the boundaries of "worldly life" and enter into the territory of "Intelligible Life" are just exceptions and the maxim is the way in which the majority of people live their life?*

In response to this question we could take some points into consideration.

First point: it is not allegedly the inherent inferiority prescribed to the human essence that human beings lack any potential for "Intelligible Life", but rendering the risky behaviors that this majority takes to satisfy their desires, would not allow anyone to charge humanity with cowardliness, lacking in disposition and potential to take the challenge of "Intelligible Life". Is it not so that to achieve dignity, wealth or social reputation these people overlook many intriguing sublunary desires and submit wholeheartedly to hardships, disdains, and even imprisonments in the hope of accomplishing any of their ideals they never refrains from any effort?

Second point: when an individual or a society takes part in "Intelligible Life", not only does it testify that all efforts it has made to be qualified for this life-style were not in vain and its movement was not towards an "impossible" destination, but having touched the new situation, that is, "Intelligible Life". It will be further attested that it has realized its true nature in the context of this new situation which was disguised before. Here, we remember a famous phrase of **Plato**:

> *Die by your will (harness your animal instincts by your will), so that to be alive by your nature – which is the eternal spirit.*[1]

"Death" in this sense doesn't imply its ordinary meaning anymore, but it is applied to the process of organization, modification and escalation of purely natural instincts into purely rational ones, which is made possible through overcoming lowly animal desires.

Third point: as we have mentioned before, although developed minds are in minority, but they are not merely exceptions, for every exception implies a counter-example of a universal law, whereas, nothing among the factors and elements of growth and perfection in a man, who has taken part in "Intelligible Life", is against his true nature. To demonstrate the legitimacy of "Intelligible Life" and to promote it as most authentic way of life, we would like to explore its natural scope, how it may be treated by people at large.

Since the majority of people are proactive; they have the capacity to learn in advance – however in a succinct manner – they would never transgress the boundaries that have been marked by societal conventions. Moreover, if our pedagogues aim to work as humanists and egalitarian, with the help of congenial social environment on one hand, and educational efforts on the other, they will be able to institutionalize respect for desired social norms as well as spiritual motivation in

---

1- This has been quoted by Sadra in Asfar.

people to actualize freedom and liberty. This is a very crucial effort without which our social history will not be evolved from natural history into a humane history.

I'd not appreciate anyone rejecting the idea impulsively. If anyone undermines human capacity, it means he has no eyes to see and witness the very existence of caravan of humanity which shines like the veins of diamond in pure natural life. Then, definitely he has the right to deny the possible positive outcomes of such efforts. We have mentioned previously, if a person or an ideology could not appreciate the phenomenon of liberty from the perspective explained above, it would not be a strong reason enough to dissuade truth inaugurating fresh human history. This universal truth is about perpetual conscious movement toward sublime perfection.

For example, if anyone is motivated to do his duties because of purely material incentives, as soon as he will be able to ascribe personal sense of duty to conscience and lofty ideals, he will find his motives the most humane and the noblest, he would proceed immediately to do his duties without thinking about whether the consciousness, movement, necessities, requirements, external and internal factors are deterministic or not?

I do not proclaim that various speculative debates, whether psychological or philosophical or of other branches of humanities should end here; they must continue their discussion, but for all the right reasons. I'd like to usher a precaution here, one must consciously begin to move towards a higher station even if he calls this process "necessity", since reality neither loves the word of "liberty", nor does it hate the word of "necessity"!

Eleven transformations

The following transformations render the evolution from "natural life" into "Intelligible Life" possible.

1. Transformation of naïve sensations into "escalated sensations/perceptions"
2. Transformation of disrupted mental streams into "an integrated system of ideas"
3. Transformation of naïve loves into "intelligible loves"
4. Transformation of chimerical hopes into "inspiring hopes"
5. Transformation of informal infatuations into "concrete love"
6. Transformation of futile arguments about perfection and goodness into "real efforts to achieve perfection and goodness"
7. Transformation of imitation and blind following into "creativity"
8. Transformation of intelligent moves of speculative reason into "wisdom seeking harmony between pure reason and moral conscience"
9. Transformation of self-indulgence and lechery into "strong will, escalated freedom and liberty".
10. Transformation of egotism and self-centeredness into "philanthropy and egalitarianism"
11. Transformation of the state of being satisfied with easily obtainable goals in life into "always searching for the better".

True Scope of Intelligible Life

Before making any effort to demonstrate the possibility of all factors of "Intelligible Life" in human life, we point it out that these possibilities have all been derived from the very knowledge of human existence as it has disclosed itself throughout history, regardless of those secondary factors which can even reduce the man into an inanimate object.

Life in its course needs instruction and management to continue to make its way through natural hindrances and obstructive human desires, and the living also want to organize their relationships with other human beings. Being conscious of the fact that "I am alive", enhancing one's understanding of various natural phenomena and other functional factors in living situations. Is it possible for any person to acquire such consciousness? If the authorities and the pedagogues of a society become determined enough to persuade the youth to develop understanding and desirability of such consciousness by role modeling it themselves, thus, demonstrating its efficacy and efficiency, the youth would not run away or turn to stones.

After creating this preliminary consciousness, comes the stage of reinforcing and gradually extending the consciousness by assimilating step by step universal values of magnificence, justice, honesty and intelligibility, both in deeds and words. The self respect and grace added with personal sense of duty, responsibility, service and philanthropy would automatically intensify the charisma attached with such transformation and it would be able to defy any amount of personal resistance or stubbornness at individual level. I wonder if anybody will object that mankind does not have the potential to develop such consciousness. If so, I cannot find any contempt worst than this accused inability to acquire this consciousness attached with human intellect.

Considering the scope of existing human social environment, well, I must remark that if the concerned authorities make honest efforts to actualize these twofold consciousnesses without having any desirable achievement, there is certainly a serious defect in the very nature of their citizens. Although we all know that this is an impossible supposition. Provided with such honest and sympathetic efforts of the authorities in a society, those who remain deprived of these two crucial consciousnesses must merely be seen as the exceptions that don't have either enough power to release themselves of the bondages of ignorance and worldly lusts or other compulsory natural factors might have deprived them of this vitality. Is it impossible to acquire the consciousness of the fact that: I am a part of a *mondus magnus* which is not a playground and moves toward a sublime telos in a completely lawful and mathematical form and I must decide my own lawful way in this teleological movement?

Indeed, the desired consciousness of intelligible life has been made accessible and convenient for us. The current belief in "natural life" is that "I can live without such consciousness". When this "I can" comes together with "consciousness is impossible", it provides a legitimate excuse for the authorities to leave their obligations in this regard! This thinking pattern must be revisited by the intelligentsia.

Before settling our scores with all deterministic and semi-deterministic forces and activities of natural life, we should clearly determine our relationship with those deterministic and semi-deterministic factors which have surrounded us? Thereafter we must see whether we have the power to actualize inherent liberty hidden deep inside our selves or not? May we interpolate a stage of growth here or we should go by it later is the most critical choice that we need to take with caution. Moreover, we need to revise our accomplishments so far on the way in order to assure ourselves that we are able to reach at least current level of self-growth on our path to "Intelligible Life".

Firstly, we should seriously take this obvious fact into consideration that the man is such a being whose life is started in complete passivity and total dependence upon others, and then slowly and gradually, his innate forces begin to be actualized. Then a time comes when, without disturbing the existing state of affairs, it begins to take advantages of the active forces, natural phenomena and human relations to construct its desirable situation, and it doesn't allow any natural event to influence it in a deterministic way.

For instance, he puts on warm clothes in winter not to catch cold. Or when he becomes sick, he seeks appropriate treatment and uses the prescribed medications to release himself of pains. If human beings would have had taken a passive stance toward deterministic and semi-deterministic factors and said that "I can't confront deterministic factors", they would have been extinguished from the planet very long time ago. While the man brilliantly makes his way against the currents of deterministic and semi-deterministic waves and extends the domain of his relations with the nature and his fellow men both qualitatively and quantitatively. You may say that this continual progress is also an effect of deterministic forces and those human qualities that have overcome the nature and redefined its relationships with "the natural" and "the human".

We say that it is a self-evident truth that the man is such a being that resists deterministic factors by its natural capacities and uses them to his own benefits in natural life. This is a truth that no wise man would deny. Thus, we'd like to endorse here that it is completely wrong to see humans as passive beings in confrontation with deterministic factors; even calling humans "passive" is the worst way of humiliating them. There is no room for doubt that when the way to progress and the necessity of it is disclosed to the man, this very disclosure, like the natural forces which the man possesses, works as a deterministic force and persuades him to move forward.

Human history is replete with such disclosures that have changed our life in all its aspects. Now the question is this: whether the man has the capability to make his way through the waves of deterministic factors by reinforcing and extending his positive capacities among conditional[1] necessities and semi-deterministic factors – which is admittedly the first step toward "Intelligible Life" – or not?! Doesn't man have the potentiality to undergo such movement? Yes, he definitely has this immense potential.

We now come to freedom and liberty. We have previously defined "Liberty" – that is the higher stage of freedom – as comprehensive self knowledge of both the positive and negative outcomes of an imperative "good" deed. In fact, the difference of "freedom" and "liberty" lies in the word of "good", since "freedom" as the ability to choose one's own way among many existing ways does not aim at "good". Now we should see if the man could be taken to the stage of "liberty" through planned instructions in an appropriate social atmosphere? Yes, the man could ascend to this stage, since as naïve senses of love in an average man could ascend to the lofty stage of intelligible love and so to be purged of earthborn lusts through preparing a positive atmosphere both at home and in society and by giving appropriate instructions again,[2] likewise we could change our naïve sense of freedom, which Rumi has compared with saddle,[3] into liberty through cultivating comprehensive self knowledge, of possible outcomes, both positive and negative, of an upcoming "good" deed and thus to *intelligiblize* human relations with desirable natural phenomena of life.

1- Conditional necessity in this context implies that there is no natural factor or phenomenon that could challenge human power as an absolute necessity.

2- Mathnavi'Ma'navi, book II, 1536-1540.

3-I am (like) an emaciated camel, and my back is wounded by my free-will which resembles a pock-saddle.

At one moment this pannier weighs heavily on this side, at another moment that pannier sags to that side.Ibid: book VI, 214-215.

This love results from knowledge—so how can

the throne be taken by a stupid man?

To love, deficient knowledge can't give birth,

But only to what's lifeless and lacks worth;

By what looks pretty it is easily stirred,

As though the true beloved's voice is heard—

Deficient knowledge can't discriminate:

The lightning with the sun it would equate.

Teaching people the necessity of this evolution is as simple and possible as teaching them the necessity of the rules of social life. People gradually become acquainted with social norms and start following them at their own pace, partly due to their nature, through formal education and/or due to other types of social influence. They feel no guilt or shame following generalized customs. However, in our case, it is possible that people may desperately try to acquit himself from the responsibility by claiming that: "I am surrounded by many deterministic factors, so I cannot act according to your norms". Therefore, whether a person is a member of ruling body or he is an average citizen, he may get punished by applying the same logic: as if someone has committed homicide, he would be told: the same deterministic law that has made you to commit homicide makes us to punish you legally too.

Influence of Intelligible Life on Human Social Living

How does "Intelligible Life" influence human society at large? In order to answer this question, we must take into account following two dimensions of intellectual evolution in the course of "Intelligible life":

1) Teleological dimension

2) Instrumental dimension.

Teleological dimension of "Intelligible Life" lies in the fact that human words, ideas and all physical and psychological activities taken in the context of "Intelligible Life" are all explained within the boundaries of that life and have no explanation outside of these boundaries, since every instance of these human affairs, according to our definition of "Intelligible Life", is a wave of life that aims at Supreme Perfection.

Even the enthusiasm that we find inside ourselves for non-intelligible goals are part of our evolutionary course of life; it is like the natural transformation through which sour grapes becomes sweet grapes and stiff internal parts of a sugarcane change into soft and juicy sugar, similarly, we are being elevated into a higher station with every new experience. This swift movement in teleological dimension of "Intelligible Life" has an instrumental appearance in natural context (L'être pour autrui) and it is essentially desired (L'être pour soi) in the context of "Intelligible Life". This teleological dimension of "Intelligible Life" is the decisive answer of every "then why" which is raised one after one.

Instrumental dimension of "Intelligible Life" would never cease to favor human beings in any point of life, since the business of "Intelligible Life" is perpetual actualization of magnificent layers of human soul; this fundamental truth is always seriously taken, which keeps this dimension dynamic and makes it a continual affair. Otherwise, if taken as a static concept it would go through numerous paradoxes difficult to counter.

These constant movements pass through many relative stations and destinations and there is no doubt that every higher state do encompass all lowers states, for higher states could not be realized but through acquisition of the lower ones.

Thus, every dimension of "Intelligible Life" becomes an instrumental dimension to render as many higher states as possible. For instance, our presence in this class at this time to discuss about "Intelligible Life" could be analyzed into two dimensions or two fundamental factors:

First dimension or factor: teleological dimension of our discussions which is an effect of conscious arrangement of deterministic and semi-deterministic appearances of nature and of our relationships with fellow men. Our personality has made various efforts to provide us with this state of affairs through envisaging an intelligible goal and choosing appropriate tools for achieving it. This state of affairs is an intelligible instance of our life. This intelligible moment is an essential part of our life that has its origin in the very phenomenon of life. This instance is a manifestation of divine word of "BE" that sprung all creatures into existence.

Second dimension or factor: our discussions in this specific time and place could be useful in leading us to legitimate ideas of our subject matter – "Intelligible Life". These legitimate ideas will render our activities, for instance, artistic activity, more intelligible, more authentic and more useful. These intelligible and authentic works of art, for example, are higher manifestations of our "Intelligible Life" which will in turn influence evolutionary cycle at concerned individual and social levels. The Holy Quran itself speaks of the necessity of this factor in "Intelligible Life":

> *Those who take the lead [in Intelligible Life]; they are those who deserve to be taken to the Divine Threshold.*[1]

Could we take such a lead in narrow and dark path of "natural life" without using good sense and pure conscience?

1-Al-Waqe'a: 10-11.

Chapter Four

The Application of Intelligible Life

This chapter examines in detail various composers to explore the scope of intelligible life in following eleven domains:

1. Psychology and personality development
2. Ethics and Morality
3. Law
4. Social Relationships
5. Science and Pursuit of Knowledge
6. Ontology
7. Weltanschauung – the World View
8. Art
9. Politics
10. Economics
11. Education

1.Psychology and Personality Development

Three aspects of personality are always important (1) inherent human potential for evolution, (II) general human participation in grand cosmic movement, and (III) altruism, a profound sense of preserving human life, i.e., having a deep sympathy inside for the suffering of living beings, of animals, of plants, and not just the human beings and their selfish commitments: its only me, myself, my family, my community, my city, my race, my religion and so on. What proves to be very significant in assuring universal unity in human individuals is their faith in being humans and what leads them to the path of interaction for mutual survival is altruism, sensing deeply the feeling of being human, and what activates all potential residing within human beings is nonetheless human personality. Let us now explore the three factors in some detail.

I. Human beings, the most exquisite creation, have an infinite scope of learning, improvement and doing the impossible. Who can deny the enormous human potential for evolution...? The ascension and transformation of a common man into a hero in many cases and in other few transcending even the nobility and piety of angels, and in turn enjoying the right of being superior to heavenly bodies bears a kind witness to the claim. This proclaimed human magnificence is not a delusion or paranoia, but the whole human history so far is a live evidence of this potential. It tells stories of people belonging to different races and nations, who have ascended to the highest pinnacle of humanity, becoming the North Stars for the rest to follow. So why should anyone believing oneself to be human should be beguiled and disheartened by the gibberish of pessimists.

II. The lowest level of achievement, i.e. personal achievements of people, is universal and regardless of their color, race and class, huge or small, people do contribute willy-nilly in continuing with the general cosmic movement.

III. Irrespective of environmental, racial, social and historical differences, all human beings, in their state of mental health, feel a kind of normative unity with respect to each other. This is not just a naïve and trivial feeling, but it is rooted deep inside human soul.

Indeed we are to commemorate and celebrate all those efforts and sacrifices that human beings give to keep up with the dignity and nobility of human life. While dealing with this invaluable human phenomenon, one should not be misled by the fake and empty slogan of *struggle for existence* raised by the fanatic votaries of power and the brokers of cruelty and oppression who say: sacrifices have all been done just for the survival and domination of mankind in natural scene. These people are either blind, or just pretend to be blind, so to disguise truth a la Machiavelli fashion. The sighs these people have uttered on sensing the oppressions and persecution that certain tribes and races have gone through do not originate from the profound sympathy with the oppressed, even when it is not in their love and interest that people should continue with their apathetic life.

When a philanthropist views an oppressed individual, group or society, the first natural wish coming into his/her hearts is: I wish such people would have never come to existence, the deprived and the destitute, an evil mark on the face of earth, the people who have nothing to enjoy in life but to tolerate such brutal oppressions and incursions. Though the wish is grounded in human sympathy, feeling bad for others' hardships and pains which torments both, who have it, and those who are witnessing the experience as bystanders, but it has to do little with saving fellow human beings from such an oppression, to end up the brutality and oppression, or having such a mature love of survival for the humanity that they actively participate in the struggle to save people from their own community to become the agents of oppression and cruelty. Such feeling is sensed through pure empathy and altruism only.

Proving the worth of an individual human personality is totally contingent upon the acceptance of "Intelligible Life". That is to say, seeing human personality as a valuable truth in light of three abovementioned principles emanate from the cause of "Intelligible Life", and not from pits of natural life. Sincerely, to understand these three principles a person needs to grow out of the corpse of "natural self" to embrace another level of human existence, to understand the sub-structural generic relationship between human beings, to fathom its value and consequently to declare each individual human personality as valuable.

"Intelligible Life" is not simply confined to the knowledge of pure existential value of individual human life, and after demonstrating the essential value of human personality – in the above mentioned three aspects– it becomes vital to view people who persistently seek development and perfection as pure manifestation of the divine providence, as the mirror of divine beauty and glory.On the contrary, the lesser the human personality counsels the moral reason and conscience, the lesser will be its value in divine scope of affairs and more will be the chance for its getting captivated by false ideals of superman, being artificially divinized more by a myth than reality, or the science fiction will take all the responsibility to create myths for itself like Batman, Spiderman or Ironman. In this manner natural human life itself is deprecated reducing itself to scientific totems and rational taboos.

2. Ethics andMorality

It is needless to say that many thoughts have been recorded in history of philosophy and religion to discuss the meaning and scope of human desirable morality in terms of its components, distinguished features and consequences. Although these ideas have many vital applications for digging deep into human intelligence and the practicality of its manifestations into variety of actions, especially those which are related to human interaction in their social context, but all of these share a common obscurity, a consequence of inability to distinguish between common sense morality of "natural life" and highly reasoned morality in "Intelligible Life". If we deal with human ideals of morality in an absolute manner without taking this distinction into account, we will undoubtedly get lost on the way.

If we look at principles of morality in the context of natural life, the following consequences will be unavoidable:

1) Ideal morality entails an unlimited scope of human tolerance, not to raise hue and cry in face of any oppression, and may continue to run the mill like Bani Israel till eternity. They will have to smile in every confronting situation to keep the cool and not to disturb the natural happenings. They will have to be totally unmindful of the reality, what type of people live and boss around them… a Pharaoh, Nero, Chengiz Khan, Teymur and Moa'vieh and/or to distinguish these from Socrates, Abuzar Ghafari, Owais Qarni and Imam Ali.

2) Ideal morality consists of acting in accordance with one's feelings and emotions while interacting with other human beings. Nevertheless, acting in accordance with personal feelings and emotions in an unconditional fashion, whether it is in harmony with the interests of other individuals and society in general or not, is diametrically in contrast with other human

principles. Suppose that there will be a significant number of cases in which acting in accordance with personal feelings and emotions will not be inconsistent with any social principle; however, if this action is merely taken by the necessity of feelings and emotions, it would be worthless, and if it is a reciprocal action, taken in the hope of being treated by others in the same way, this would be nothing but moral merchandizing.

3) Ideal morality may comprise acting upon a chain of principles insulated by ruling authorities into some legal frameworks; although such moral principles serve as potent moral agent in the society by providing a working ethics, realistically speaking, they are an effect of particular genetic, historical, racial, economic and cultural background. This is indeed the case with all human societies; every culture in general has a particular style of thinking and acting on its own having its origin in a particular kind of socio-environmental necessity and motives. It is certainly consistent with our previous comment that ideal moral actions and conducts signified as valued behaviors are celebrated in each society and their actors are the heroes, the stars defining the collective conscience of that society. Such people and their humane values are of an absolute significance, for the respective society and for the humanity as a whole.

4) Ideal morality is the housemaid of legal norms! Indeed, natural life and its worldly aims have worked best not only to develop a deep sense among the common to view and regard the morality as means to enforce laws, reduce crime and personal offense of people against their fellow men. It may have helped them to cut their judiciary budgets, but we witness an ever rising graph of ordinary crimes in the most developed nation. This so called ideal morality appears to be a phony claim for peaceful social coexistence, but its complete negligence to teach human reason to stay away from immorality is an unforgivable misbehavior, especially when

many reasons becoming the eventual cause of immorality, alcoholism, homosexuality and adultery are not banished from society. Aren't we trying to be hypocritical, when we entice people to embark natural life, don't we know the ark has a hole at the bottom, and it will sink in the middle of sea.

Morality in "Intelligible Life" consists of:

1) Seeing oneself as a part of the whole - human life - which Holy Spirit has breathed into us:

And I breathed into him of my spirit...[1]

To accept the fact that our relationship with other human beings is like the relationship that exists between the parts of a spirit or like the relationship that various colors have with each other when they are refracted by prism into many though they are emitted by a single ray.[2]

If one sets the categorical imperative – one must do what one expects other to do in a similar situation – at the very point of departure only, he will be able to taste "Intelligible Life". Since we know, this is the very imperative that practical judgment and pure conscience invite us to follow good life, and this is not possible unless we come out of natural life and enter into "Intelligible Life". Since this morality is dynamic and purposeful, it could not lose its substance by being unconcerned with social events. This morality sees the society through a lofty perspective, as Muhammad (SAW) had invited us and Imam Ali (peace be upon him) see us all pacing on the prescribed divine path.

1- Al-Hijr: 29.

2-Unless this element or divine ray loses the course that the God has determined for it to preserve its primordial nature; as we have noted at the end of previous section.

2) Having screened human emotions thoroughly and accepting the necessity of saturating them in an intelligible manner, this morality builds itself upon escalated emotions according to the ever enduring ethics of human societies, the quoted principles are not imprisoned in isolated compartments, but they are compatible with both public and personal phenomena of the living and encompass whole life.

In sum, carnal emotions are the basic drive of human life, therefore, they are indispensible for morality in "Intelligible Life", but the ultimate telos of "Intelligible Life" resides in participating in the holistic cosmic movement, thus morality could not rely on basic raw emotions only. They might be the spice of life but they must be seasoned well; we eat cooked not raw anymore.

3) Morality in "Intelligible Life" is a conscious and deliberate choice for a certain quality of life; it is not an autonomous activity spontaneously occurring in the natural stream occasioned by a social life in a given society. Then the dilemma lies in the right cognition of a moral and immoral society. Seeing one's acts in accordance with prevailing social norms do not raise question of a superior morality, as described above in case of alcoholism, fornication and adultery etc. But remaining totally oblivious either of such an absolute morality, even while staying away from the prevailed customs of an immoral society, runs the high risk of repressing human conscience, keeping it jailed under the license of prefabricated social frameworks unable to liberate itself and live a free and authentic life.

What is possible in morality and what should occur naturally rather than indoctrinated by some authority is still a shrouded mystery for the common man. Alas! Many of us keep wandering in the desert of natural desire but no alchemist meets us and no holy spirit engulfs us saving our souls from ruining. What is a mirage: an ideal moral life without a free conscience or substituting conscience with consciousness? What is to be done with common perception that the pure conscience – source of human knowledge for goodness and perfection and the main driving force to achieve these – is nothing more than a delusion? Therefore, we should either deny human ideal morality, or declare the human free conscience a serious necessity. It is only within the context of "Intelligible Life" that the necessity of not just free but independent conscience becomes sensible.

4) Morality in "Intelligible Life" could not be reduced to a housemaid of law in natural life or a means for reducing crime and judiciary costs, although it is one of the functions of morality in "Intelligible Life" to decide for social norms and draw legal frameworks to ensure that these norms are practiced to live purely a natural life. Such practical morality which is designed to appeal to the reason motivates people to elevate their morality, not for the sake of blind following but for their own satisfaction; it is the moral and spiritual satisfaction which reduces crime rate and judiciary costs and not the satisfaction of basic physical needs.

In simpler words, we need to look for the real objectives, for instance, cool wind is one of the natural consequences of irrigating a farm, but a farmer always farms for the harvest not for cool wind. We should not make by-products our aim, thus it is not a "free" but an independent conscience that results from practicing higher morality, a conscience which is not chained to lower nafs, i.e. seeking satisfaction of primary needs and freedom in making choices of lower order, such as what will be the menu of my dinner table, or what brand I will select for my shoes or dress, or in which part of town I'd like to reside, and in satisfaction of these desires he/she may jeopardize higher order morality, such as indulging into corruption, or using other unfair means to satisfy these desires which apparently look quite natural and harmless. Moreover, considering the sense of guilt and shame that is attached with corrupting morals, where is the freedom, what powers are left with this free conscience? Can it liberate itself from the pain of guilt and shame that gnaws at the heart of wrong doers and sinners? Will it be able to reduce the doubts and skepticism that make each breath difficult to inhale and exhale? Can it ensure sense of self respect and autonomy that a fair and just person enjoys within oneself? So what is worth attention: a free conscience raising doubts, anxiety and frustration in life or an independent conscience that can envision the outcomes of the outcomes of one's action and thus choose wisely?

Morality in the context of "Intelligible Life" is more authentic and magnificent than being actually realized, if natural morality is the medicine for social pains and ills, the higher morality is the hygiene that keeps us healthy, safely protected from pains and ailments. The relationship between morality and "Intelligible Life" is indeed like the relation that exists between body and soul, the mind and the spirit. Therefore, the prophetic claim of Muhammad (SAW) declares perfection and marks his finality in this claim:

> *I have been sent to complete moral virtues.*

Why because it does not ensure just medicine it provides a complete regime for hygiene as well for social ills and issues that can arise in a society.

If we compare the above mentioned prophetic statement with the following verses of Holy Quran:

> *Whoever does good whether male or female and he is a believer, we will most certainly make him live a happy life.*[1]

1-Al-Nahl: 97.

...Surely my prayer and my sacrifice and my life and my death are (all) for Allah, the lord of the worlds.[1]

We will happily conclude that "Intelligible Life" which is competent enough to be attributed to the Lord and could be called "Happy Life" is founded on those human lofty moral virtues that the Holy Prophet (SAW) has been sent to complete.

3.Law

Law within the context of "Intelligible Life" could not content itself with discovering and regulating natural but societal life based relationships of human beings for coexistence. "Intelligible Life" attaches at least the same importance to human spiritual rights as natural rights to satisfy physical needs.

The only task that law in ordinary sense has been in charge of until this time was to prevent people not to tear each other down! Whether or not law has been able to preserve this basic human right to survive in peace has been accomplished successfully across various regions of world and diverse human societies is debatable; and complete agreement or disagreement in this case would be controversial.

Nevertheless, all legal frameworks and judicial systems that have been ordained to ensure peace and justice have so far been aiming at preparing the society for a peaceful coexistence, without having any concern over human normative necessities. AsRobert Jackson, an American Justice, says:

American law has no concern over moral duties. In fact, an American citizen could act totally legal, while being a morally corrupted person.[2]

1-Al-Ana'm: 162.

2-Law in Islam, Herbert J. Lisbani: Preface.

This is not merely a characteristic of American law, but it is applicable to every law that has been enacted to facilitate social coexistence. If the legislators of these laws were truly concerned about moral evolution, independent conscience and supremacy of human compassion over other emotions our natural history marked by human blood here and there would have certainly been a more kind and humane history.

It is such a sad story that even common laws legislated by different governments are religiously practiced in times of peace, but as soon as some crisis, such as natural disasters like earth quake or flood, or unnatural like war, economic meltdown, or any other form of political upheavals strike the society, the laws are floundered as if they were a dirty piece of paper, and human beings take no time to turn into wild beasts.

As we have mentioned previously, these laws even in their strongest forms are like magnificent edifices that are built on the top of a volcano. The human beings whose "natural self" have not been tilled for "Intelligible Life" are the volcanoes that are responsible for ruining themselves and everything that has been built upon them.

Since human beings have a short lifetime, therefore, the ruinous destructions caused by such volcanoes may not offer are a tangible experience for everyone. Such incidents are not part of everybody's conscious memory; nevertheless, each trauma becomes part of the collective unconscious of that society. To get acquainted with these destructions, we just need to catch a glimpse of the history. To add insult to the injury, people try to justify the loss in name of abject fatalism, that such happenings were the natural consequences of chaotic situations like war and political transitions, thus are unavoidable and they have nothing to do with erupting volcanoes – human beings losing control over their natural selves.

There is no doubt that every unusual event in society lead necessarily to legal vacuum and thus to social chaos. But the question here is natural: whether the particular social chaos is necessarily an outcome of those unusual events or it is vice versa? Alas! In whatever direction we may look in the mirror, the picture remains the same; with pure shame and guilt we recognize the gruesome face of barbaric instincts reining our natural life which is barely hidden under the mask of carefully designed legislature. Unfortunately, the colors of this mask are so temporary, that are blown away in one quick wash. What does the naked face of humanity speaks of: human made laws have no role in building human character or a truly humane self. That is why "Intelligible Life" insists on the patronage of divine laws of rules and procedures governing everyday life processes. The rules and procedures may keep changing with emerging needs of time, but the divine spirit should stay the same. In this way people get acquainted with spiritual excellences, and take the opportunity to get benefited of the intelligible life.

It seems that jurists are either not keen explorers, or powerful agents of change; therefore they choose gently to succumb to the deficiencies of existing laws coded to protect natural life-style customized for a society. However, may be in their dreams, they should try to revisit the moral excellences coded in traditional laws and find ways to incorporate them into present legal systems.

If anyone says that it is hard to harmonize traditional morality and practical reason with governing laws, then future of morality and safety of mankind rests at the mercy of God. Why...? If there is no one to lead the ark, it will never sail and the shores of time can be as unfriendly as ever. Every intelligent mind is well aware of the fact that moral decline in society is more fatal than temporary protests of corrupted people. When people keep their mouths tightly zipped, humanity fells victim to the mercy of dumb law and blind justice waiting in cold-blooded silence, whether or not the fate favors the right of their spiritual freedom.

Law in "Intelligible Life", however, is a function of human nature's real necessities and thus is evolutionary in its nature; along with the necessities arising from the nature of individual physical and social life, it introduces other necessities as well that arise from ascending nature of human beings. In doing so not only it tries to show us the concrete outcomes of the pursuit of these necessities, but it is also attempts to reorganize the necessities of natural life based on a correct logic.

4. Social Relationships

"Intelligible Life" has undertaken the momentous task of changing utility-based human relations into purely humane relations. Utility-based relations either originate in embarrassing Hobbesian formula of "*Homo homoni lupus*" or alternatively may lead to it.

We keep emulating the idol of natural life, trying to cool down its fury by slaying our natural desire for justice and self-respect at its altar and we concoct epics to magnify the glory of our failure to keep the genie locked up. Shall we wake up from this nightmare to heartening awareness that "Intelligible Life" has the capacity to transform our skin saving utilitarian relationships into endurable humane relations and it is not merely an amiable illusion, but a reachable truth? Suffice it is to catch a glimpse of the history of sacrifices that have been given to uphold truth and justice. Such a perspective of history introduces us with saints and martyrs, such remarkable stalwarts of human history that have gone beyond every limit of self-centeredness and utilitarianism.

Furthermore, if we remove all phrases about human moral excellences and all tales of purely humane relations from our classical literature, history and anthropological masterpieces, there will be nothing more left to fascinate us in those black words written in pale white background. We want to read the classics voraciously but in search of humane characters and are moved by them, we laugh with them and we weep and mourn with them. It is certified, hence, that we want and we have the capacity for keeping purely humane relations.

When we read in a literary work, for instance, that a person has compromised with all of his personal interests and has undergone lot of suffering to uphold a truth or have submitted to some service on the call of his conscience, we are filled with the sense of greatness. We idealize that person as hero. Indeed, there is nothing in this world more valuable than life, but how powerful is the pull of this conscience, what is charisma attached with it that people happily give their lives away, e.g. for protecting one's family, community or country. Thus, the very idea that social relations could not be established upon anything but personal utility is a kind of self-delusion.

What binds the relationship between a student and a teacher, the student fee and teacher's salary? A conscientious professor would like to keep his relationship with his students beyond the walls of a classroom, even after his duty hours, listening to the call of his duty. He'd endeavor to sneak into the depths of their minds and souls. On the other hand, students could see their professor as the mirror of reality helping them to roam around in garden of wisdom. What is an absolute necessity...?

Generally speaking, members of a caravan aiming at a common destination need to share only the necessity of arriving at that destination. This is why "Intelligible Life" regards the knowledge of the "Ultimate Telos of Life" vital for all human beings. This realization and sense of duty has kept intellectuals on their toes, taking the pain to deliver knowledge, thus, awakening human lives to pure consciousness and what has agonized and tormented them is the indifference of people towards true knowledge. They are bewildered at common narrow-mindedness: how could people be so satisfied with their temporary relationships in life that a slight disturbance would move them to ideas of homicide or genocide and how ignorant they are about their permanent relations with the Creator and how negligent they are in their obligations towards creation.

To *intelligiblize* our social relations, thus, we need to understand the essence and necessity of "Ultimate Telos of Life" in a very empathetic manner.

5. Science and Pursuit of Knowledge

Consciousness is the building block of "Intelligible Life". It means that the human being is a living being whose life must be managed by him to be flourished in all its possible aspects. Management in this sense would not be possible without being conscious of the nature, other human beings and possible socio-individual relations. Moreover, the man is such a being by his nature enthusiastically desires to know even of very trivial and seemingly insignificant issues. Being in direct contact with realities which overtures them is, thus, necessary.

There is no difference between "Purely Natural Life" and "Intelligible Life" in this respect. But the question of life is not restricted to this issue, since it is needless to say that knowing realities is one thing and organizing an intelligible relation with them is another thing. As our knowledge of the vital necessity of food for human being does not feed anyone, writing hundreds of volumes of justice will not bring it to society unless we decide to reorganize our socio-individual relation based on justice.

"Intelligible Life" warns science not to be misused by natural self.

It is needless to say that science in its general sense has two objectives:

1. Actualizing a human potential in contact with reality, i.e. human knowledge of scientific facts unearths his latent existential abilities, and at the same time enables him to get benefited from them. To state the matter differently, knowledge brings power. The better we are in contact with reality, the more empowered we feel to get things done in the right way.

2. Objectification of science, like a building which objectifies the architectural sciences.

"Intelligible Life" does not deny any of these objectives, but it considers both of them necessary with regard to the reality of life. The most significant issue in intelligible paradigm of science is essentially teleological. Why these objectives must be fulfilled?The naturalists' answer to this question is very clear. Both of these objectives are met to preserve "as it is" the natural conditions of life at any cost mindless of any change required. This is the logic of natural life rephrased in due respect of a semi-philosophical claim that man has no essence other than allowed by history.

Thus conceived, all knowledge pursuits carried out by science focus arounddevelopment of our natural disposition, most common of which is our speculative reason. It is not the most desired but the most natural outcome of our expectations with science. The saddest part of this development is that naturalist paradigm of science has gravely reduced the most dynamic being, the human beings into multiple natural aspects with its shallow scientism and by doing so it has even disarranged his natural dispositions.

Is it not a sign of disorganization of human natural disposition that certain political and social influence may try blatantly to repress consciousness by using powerful narcotics seducing people into eternal slavery and be successful? Isn't the dominance of Machiavellianism in global discourse of power a strong cause for a venomous dismantling ofsignificant human natural dispositions?

Although "Intelligible Life" admits the crucial role of these two goals in defining science, but it mainly seeks to find the purpose and orientation of these goals. "Intelligible Life" asks: What should be the desired outcome of these goals? What do people want? This "want" is the compass that sets the direction of human life in any movement. Whether the objectives of this important human "want" should be a trivial, temporary and ordinary physical phenomenon, prescribed by the shallowness of naturalism, as we witness people conditioned to petty desires, repeating in their everyday sentences: "I want to go to cinema", "I want to buy that shirt" and "I want to taste that chocolate". The social and natural sciences may attempt to analyze it objectively into several factors that may have caused the expression of "I want" generating an eternal paradox: how could a subjective matter be so well understood objectively? In any case, the most significant fact is that this "I want" has a distinguished place of its own in the general cosmic order. **Sheikh Mahmud Shabestari** reminds us:

> *If you move a grain of its place*
>
> *the world will collapse fast*

"Intelligible Life" is to *intelligiblize*(i.e. realize on intelligible basis) this "I want" by intellection and free conscience. *Intelligibilization* of "I want" in this sense consists of reducing it into divine will, i.e. developing understanding of cause and effect according to divine cosmic rules rather than natural principles. Thus conceived, science within the context of "Intelligible Life" must promote human autonomy as a divine being. This divinized science will finally fill the gap that ideological disputes have brought about between the domains of "Is-ness" and "Ought-ness".

6. Ontology

Undoubtedly, it is only the "Intelligible Life" that could mirror both faces of the world of existence, i.e., "natural (phenomenal) aspect of the world" and "transcendental (noumenal) reality of the world".

1. Phenomenal aspect of the world consists of those phenomena, relations and dimensions that are measurable by our five ordinary senses. Scientific research, both qualitative and quantitative, inquires into the issues and problems from various points of view in attempt to describe the issues or seek solutions. This aspect of the world is totally dependent on our perceptions, and it is unconcerned with soul and spiritual problems.

Besides the empirical evidence that logically demonstrates the objective reality of the world, which is understood by using various faculties of our mind, there exists a world, which is independent of the logical boundaries constructed by human mind.

Quran has reiterated several times to recognize the existence of that inner world, which constitutes the reality of "Intelligible Life". [Shall I repeat some verses from the Quranic Chapters of Ar-Rahman, Al-Isra, and Kahf?] If that's not enough, you can yourself explore the seven hundreds verses to seek sufficient evidence to establish what is emphasized in Holy Quran:

Doesn't it clearly state: God is the sole creator of the world, and human beings must seek knowledge about the world and the universe around thoroughly and try to get benefited by this knowledge in their course of development and observe growth in world here and hereafter. God reveals his signs both in "external world" and "internal world":

> We will soon show them our signs in the universe and in their own souls.[1]

2. Transcendental reality of the world is cognized by the God alone and this noumenal aspect of the world is a manifestation of the "Sphere of Divine Command":

Surely his is the creation and the command[2]

The relation of transcendental and material aspects of the world is like the relationship of soul and body. The Noumenal aspect of the world is the soul and the world is the manifestation of Divine Providence.

Thus conceived, the world, even in its noumenal form, does not have any independent existence or reality; therefore, most people restrict their studies to the phenomenal aspect of life, at the most they get to know what the relationship between God and the world is. Nevertheless, phenomenal world is, indeed, an objective manifestation of the transcendental reality of the world. If we see the phenomenal world through the prism of "Intelligible Life" – which is undoubtedly the source of transcendental understanding – we will easily understand the contingent nature of the phenomenal world. Perhaps those who have described the phenomenal world as "illusion", "shadow",

---

1-Fussilat: 53.
2- Al-Araf: 54.

"bubble" and so on, have been successful to see the world from an intelligible point of view, but certainly they have been wrong in their negative description of the world, since as we have said previously: the world has objective reality.

If we cannot have an intelligible vision of reality, where both material and immaterial dimensions are accommodated in an intelligible fashion, we may fall into various kinds of dualism, e.g. Platonism (*ideas* and *appearances*), Aristotelianism (*matter* and *form*), Kantianism (*das ding an sich* and *das ding für sich*) and Hegelianism (*the object* and *the subject*), which have deprived us of an integral understanding of the world and its totality – the unity of perception.

7. Weltanschauung – World View

Taking snapshots of both the internal and external worlds is one aspect, and trying to get a comprehensive knowledge of the world and the place of human self in it through all possible cognitive means is another issue. To put the matter differently, a mirror that could show us the history of cosmos in a random way without giving any explanation of its course is essentially different from an integrated worldview that is able to distinguish between mathematical and aesthetic aspects of reality and analyze them in a logical way, without losing sight of the possibility of change in its stance by virtue of environmental variables.

On the other hand, one episode of a serial, regardless of its length and complexity, is not able to foretell the quality of next episodes, let alone to be able to provide enough material for its comprehensive evaluation.

From the very dawn of the history of human knowledge, nevertheless, there were many people who have claimed for themselves different titles such as "ontologist", "philosopher" or "sophist". They seem to have a unitary claim that they are able to understand and judge every episode of the serial, whereas, they are distinguished parts of just a single episode of the serial, although they had some knowledge of what has preceded them, yet all of them were totally oblivious of what was to follow, in terms of theories, principles and values even in their own respective discipline. However, at least some of them did acknowledge that:

> O' breath of phenomenal existence, whatsoever words thou mayest utter/ know that thereby thou hast bound another veil upon it.
>
> That utterance and that state of existence are the bane of spiritual perception/ to wash away blood with blood is absurd, absurd.[1]

Then, what we should do? What could be the logical base on which the episode of a serial has put such consequential claim in the sphere of weltanschauung?

The answer of this question is what we have said earlier in this section: taking snapshots of the internal and external worlds is one thing and trying to get a comprehensive knowledge of the world and the place of human self in it through all possible cognitive means is another.

When we say that human being is able to have a comprehensive knowledge of the world both externally and internally, we are speaking of an *objective* cognitive possibility in human being, and not of a delusion, since if you ask the aforementioned philosophers of their worldview, although they do know better than anyone else that they are just one episode of reality among numerous other existing episodes, they will

---

1- Mathnavi'e Ma'navi, book III, 4724-4726.

say that we have discovered the universal laws and concepts through which we could interpret the world in its totality.

Therefore, man does not merely take snapshots of the reality but he has indeed a comprehensive knowledge of the gamut of reality which enables him to interpret it as a totality. Thus conceived, *Weltanschauung* will necessarily lead us to the idea that there is a Divine Providence in this world that moves it toward the sublime destination – which is the core of "Intelligible Life" – by means of eternal laws, since all episodes of reality are so intertwined that form an irreducible unity.

8. Art

We have already discussed of Art and Aesthetics in full length in a treatise under the title of *"The Philosophy of Art from an Islamic Point of View"*.[1]We have already described that there are three basic theories of art: I) art for art; II) art for humanity; III) art for humanity in the intelligible life. In dealing with the third theory, we have defined the meaning of life and a meaningful life as:

> *The realization of human self and ideals within the parameters of intelligible life are based on eternity as the only passage to spiritual actualization.*

The meaningful life which is one and the same with "Intelligible Life" consists of:

> *A conscious life which canalizes deterministic and pseudo-deterministic forces and other activities of natural life into the course of evolutionary goals through the development of liberty which flourishes in human will as it would assist*

1-An extended version of this treatise has been posthumously published under the title of *"Aesthetics and Art from an Islamic Point of View"* by M. T. Jafari.

> *human self, which is gradually formed in this process, to realize the Ultimate Telos of Life. This Ultimate Telos of Life is participation in general cosmic movement toward Supreme Perfection.*

Art for humanity within the parameters of "Intelligible Life" is, thus, imagining the "reality as it is" in conjunction with the "reality as it ought to be" through human escalated (transcendentalized) perceptions.Art within the context of "Intelligible Life" does not only appear as bondage but it depicts the deterministic and pseudo-deterministic forces of natural life as means of self-liberalization. Thus conceived, the work of art liberalizes human selves from the deterministic and pseudo-deterministic bondages and prepares them to participate in the grand cosmic movement. Every work of art that appears under the inspiration of "Intelligible Life", is not only emotionally effective in the context of natural life, but it is itself a wave of "Intelligible Life" that has the ultimate capacity to *intelligiblize* the society. Since "Intelligible Life" is essentially dynamic and cultivates all emerging phenomena in the course of human development, seeing art as a wave of it will surely secure it from being misused by inhuman schools to uproot human consciousness, liberty and purposefulness.

9. Politics

It is needless to say that there is no such controversial word (conceptually and practically) as "Politics" in human discourse. If we are to define "Politics" a la *conscious* intellectuals those who take human reality into prime consideration, we will define it as: "organizing human lives in a way that may assist them to achieve the noblest material and spiritual goals". But if we take the actual practice of ordinary politicians into consideration – that unfortunately includes the majority of politicians around the globe – we will encounter with many shameful events. Politics in this sense reduces "Some-ones" into "Some-things".

The fact that politics does always move in a paradoxical manner may only seem wonderful to those who are not familiar with the *reality* of "Natural Life", while politics appears wonderful to conscious people only when it is devoid of any paradox. It is indeed wonderful, for when life has no plan to reconstruct itself on the basis of human ideals there will be naturally no hope to experience it in any other shape. Now, if you are going to pass the reins of social affairs of people to these politicians, you should accept it in advance as natural that they will *surely* see people as just "moving things".

This is not a narrow-minded pessimistic approach to politics. It is purely based on political facts. If you are to approach this harsh reality yourself, you should go to a library in your vicinity and borrow **Machiavelli**'s *"Prince"* or you must listen to professional politicians for few minutes.[1]

The argument is made very clear here and does not require any further explanation. Didn't I already know how logical could be Machiavellianism within the parameters of naturalism…? After all, Machiavelli interprets all human affairs from purely natural point of view. This is why many philanthropists so remorselessly criticize him. His writings appear phony and self descriptions of reality when he bitterly fails to ascend above his personal vision of life instead of exploring the scope of human life in context of unfathomable human potential and infinite possibilities to use this potential.

1-It is needless to say that we are not to beat all politicians with the same stick, since we do not deny the very existence of those honorable politicians who has toiled and sacrificed to change "some-things" into "some-ones". We do send our warmest greetings to all those noble politicians of the past and at the present time.

Machiavelli's objective is to change natural life into an earthly paradise (golden cage) that dissuades the flight to heaven of the passionate seekers.

On a devilish note, I dare to remark: why we must reduce our paradise to the offerings of Machiavelli...? Why not create one of your own choice?

On the contrary, politics within the context of "Intelligible Life" has all essential levels: it has been given purpose, point of departure and destination. Its meaning and purpose implies preparing the vision forconscious life which canalizes deterministic and pseudo-deterministic forces of natural life into the course of evolutionary goals through the development of liberty which flourishes in human will. Its point of departure is breaking the golden cage of self-love and bringing the life back to its original track. And its destination is the Ultimate Telos of Life [Supreme Perfection]. If a politician says: "it is impossible, contrary to our past experience, which are evident of the fact that human beings have the capacity for no other living style but natural", he is undoubtedly either unaware of true human nature, or he is just lying a la Machiavelli.

Is it not so that the similar human beings have struggled time and again to achieve higher dignities in natural life dauntingly and have been unyielding to all superficial ideas and life-styles? Is it not so that mankind has sacrificed incredibly to realize the ideals of truly humane "natural self"? Are we not talking about the people who have used their mental faculties creatively and passionately to catch that flimsy flame called "Ishq"?

Alas! If most of the human potential would have been used in service of the "Intelligible Life" in a better organized and comprehensive fashion, the history of our natural life would have been transformed into humane history a very long time ago. Sooner it will be achieved, if our politicians realize that their *mission* is to change "Some-things" into "Some-ones".

10. Economics

If we are to study economic issues, one of the prime necessities of human life within the parameters of "natural life", "self-preservation" and "self-love" are the fundamental features of humanity as defined by the naturalists. According to them these issues are fundamental for human existence, hence not only we have to recognize their importance, we have to offer them absolute ownership. To tell you the truth, either we do not possess the necessary knowledge, or we are lacking in comprehension of the term "self-preservation" in the real context of natural life. Therefore, we always regard it a trivial issue that psychologists and philosophers entertain themselves with!

We should not be so negligent to the topic; keeping in view the racist claims of the naturalists, the issue of ownership can be very well manipulated and diabolically monopolized by the elitist mindset of the world. There will appear new Lords on the earth, masters of the fate in some societies, who will not mind getting rid of "unwanted" people on earth. After all, this world is for the chosen people, so what about the rest? Let them be exiled to other planets!

The obsession for "Self-preservation" if went out of control may provoke the protagonists of "survival of the fittest" to wage war to claim absolute ownership of the economic resources of this world, though it appears to be a hallucinatory idea now. In order to correct their vision and keep sanity of the world intact, we must introduce naturalists into the true life – Intelligible Life. They must look at the grand picture of life, to avoid the mania getting further deteriorated into wildness;

flashes have suddenly begun to appear in various regions of world by waging "War of Terror". Now it is no more a game of stifling pleasures, or reducing the aim of life to satisfaction of few natural needs. The "golden cage" is already full of people charged of over-doing and victimizing others.

Having taken into account the dreadful voraciousness of human ownership, we sense a natural need of a guard to protect us from this dragon. We say that the guardian of mankind in the issue of ownership may also be the guardian of his life, respect and happiness. Isn't it asking for too much? If we seek protection by force, the Armed forces of the world are themselves bogged down in the swamp of naturalism, and are not familiar with different kinds of life style as proposed by us. What they can ensure at maximum is peaceful social co-existence, so their natural efforts would end up in short term gains. It means that modernity can only be maintained by force in natural life. Where will we find such compassionate, honest and just humanitarian souls, who would save the weak from being culled by the powerful? We may only wish for the return of the divine soul, to safeguard life on earth.

Truly speaking the epic of natural life as narrated by the naturalists themselves are clearly evident of the fact that the most valuable potential of human beings, whether mental or physical, has always been wasted by this diabolic temptation that: "everything is my personal property and everyone around falls under my means to satisfy myself". On the contrary, "Intelligible Life" tell us that every human being has the right to live with equal respect and share the same resources. This right by no means be manipulated by the la Machiavelli egotists.

To defend human lives from unprecedented aggression of egotists and pathological dictators, we need to undertake some heroic tasks as follows:

1. To replace "self-preservation" with altruism, i.e., instead of violating others' right to live, promote mutual sustainability of life, that the right to live is not an individual claim of a person, tribe or nation, but every living human being has a universal claim for this divine bounty.
2. To view each and every mental and physical step taken in this direction as "moments" in grand cosmic movement.
3. To consider all economic resources as means to serve the life and the living and not vice versa.

Thus conceived, economic management in every society could be conducted thoroughly in an intelligible fashion. It would be visible only, if we start viewing ourselves as waves of the sea of "Intelligible Life" and understand that our interests are eternally intertwined.

It is evident enough that economic development within the parameters of "Intelligible Life" is wholly contingent upon the concept of "*nicht-Ich*". The unappeasable sense of absolute ownership will vanish only when the man enters into the sphere of "Intelligible Life".

It may be argued that such a visionary economic planning can be done by the people who live in fantasy rather than reality; maybe such dreamers don't even deserve to live on this planet. Whom I should listen to ... these cocoons... who have ears but to listen to themselves only, or should I turn my face to spiritual master Rumi, who recommends to bargain such ears for better ones?[1] Alas! Human economic conditions would not be reformed, because "sermons are utopian" and no ear has

---

1- In such cases Rumi prefers to sting our souls with his heavenly words may we lend an ear to the truth:
Sell those dumb ears and buy better ones/ for donkey's ears are just for simpletons! (Spiritual Couplets, book I: 1033)

been given to these, neither in the past, nor today and will not be given in future.

I'd plainly remark: this objection is overruled. The bargain is very simple: lend your ears to sweet tunes and get in the "golden cage" with weapons of mass destruction to safeguard; listen to the bitter truth, sow in your heart, and till the land until you reap a rose garden. It is ridiculous to say "we could not have a morally conditioned economy!" Life is a unified whole and both economy and ethics are parts of it. We cannot let any part fall apart from us.

Of course, I do not know at present how we should *intelligiblize* the economy (or conceptualize the matter on intelligible basis)! But my personal inability in this regard does not render this task impossible, since human history is replete with the sacrifices that have been made for such human noble ideals as "freedom", "justice", "knowledge" and so forth.

11. Education[1]

Education within the parameters of "Intelligible Life" is viewed as natural progression. It involves, training of perception and enhancement of other mental faculties, such as creativity and problem solving amongst youth, so that they may enter into learning of the practical realities of life from the very beginning, and they move gradually but authentically through the stages of "naturalistic lifestyle" and then finally enter into the realm of "Intelligible Life".

It may be argued that how can we make education system so

1- For more on this issue see 'The Fundamentals of Education" written by Allama Jafari. This book has been published by the Allama Jafari Institute in Tehran in 2011. Allama Jafari has eloquently applied the principles of intelligible life in the context of Education. (Translator) authentic and in this sense comprehensive for the youth of a society whose adults are bogged down in the swamp of naturalism.[1] Honestly, it is really hard task but we must endure it if we are to realize the "Intelligible Life".

When we say that it is the task of education to transform human beings, whether the young or the adults or even the old, from "natural life" into the realm of "Intelligible Life", we do not expect that any existing formal education would produce Avicenna within some days or few years but we cannot even deny the possibility of getting one in coming generations. The critical point here is that we must ensure our pupils that the materials and methods they will graduate in are based upon pure scientific logic, all they have to add is personal interest and hard work; whatever they wish to become does not lie beyond the scope of natural intelligence they are endowed with.

The loss of time and energy for indulging in futile debates by the intelligentsia and intellectual authorities of the society leads to two negative outcomes, the loss of interest and motivation of people in "Intelligible Life" and their penchant satisfaction of staying comfortably in the "Natural Life"; consequently, intellectual evolution is paused in the society. Isn't it indeed greatest loss not only of a society but of mankind as a whole? It is the duty of social authorities and pedagogues to pay earnest attention to this consequence. Is it not so that the principle of Telesis is a fundamental aspect of human life? Is it not so that we – humans – always act purposefully regardless of the host of necessities hovering around us to captivate?

Thus, purposefulness is a generic characteristic of human actions. "Intelligible Life" advocates, that one should choose those goals, which are more compatible with one's natural

---

1- See more about this in the previous chapter of the book (i.e. Part B).

temperament. However, in any case, a personwill have to undergo eleven-folded transformations thoroughly to reach the ultimate station of "Intelligible Life", regardless of the fact whether or not his/her temperament is congenial for intelligible life. Otherwise, we can safely observe that people are on their path toward actualization. Teaching people about the significance of seeking some higher objectives in life definitely implies basic understanding of the principle of Telesis and developing the ability to differentiate between the goals of everyday mundane life and the higher purpose – The Ultimate Telos, i.e. authentic and truth-seeking activities in accordance with divine laws.

All conscious men and women naturally desire to find an answer for the question: "what is the ultimate objective of life?" without which life would undoubtedly be swamped into nothingness. The challenge resides in identifying a correct objective in the first place and a universal objective in the last. It is not that easy as to make the workers of an industry realize, why the industrialist wants them to labor so hard. Even if they come to understand, their individual understanding at various departmental levels may be unique, different and not matching with each other.

Similarly, when pedagogues go in search for answers in their respective societies, the answers received may be difficult, incomprehensive and too abstract in their nature, as mentioned in the 1st chapter. So what one should do? Leave this search for ever? Let people live in the stinky swamps they have created for themselves…? Or continue to search for the Ultimate Telos of Life until and unless all people in world agree to live an "Intelligible Life."

EPILOGUE

One of the most important challenges issued by the critique of Orientalism and Eurocentrism in the humanities and social sciences is to identify and develop ideas that are rooted in non-western knowledge traditions. A serious and reasonable approach to this task would not consider eliminating or marginalizing Western thought. Instead, it would consider Western thought as one of the many knowledge traditions which in the modern period happens to be a globally hegemonic one. The problem with this hegemony is that it tends to marginalize or silence other civilizational voices that have the potential to yield concepts that would be of use for the humanities and social sciences. The project, therefore, is one of searching for ideas that originate in non-Western traditions that are hitherto unknown or undeveloped in the modern human sciences. This work of Allama Jafari, *Intelligible Life*, provides us with an example of how ideas from the Islamic tradition may contribute to an understanding of the modern world.

The works of nineteenth century thinkers such as Karl Marx, Max Weber, Emile Durkheim, Sigmund Freud, Harriet Martineau and others addressed the big question of the nature of modern society, its ills and discontents, and the prospects of a successful redress of its problems. Unfortunately, the thought of a host of non-Western scholars such as José Rizal from the Philippines, Said Nursi from Turkey, Ali Shari'ati from Iran, Pramoedya Ananta Toer from Indonesia, Syed Hussein Alatas from Malaysia, and numerous other scholars from around the world were hardly ever regarded as containing authoritative commentaries on the nature of modern life. Their works were, and continue to be, relegated to area studies and not seen as having universal significance. It is important, therefore, to seriously consider a thinker like Allama Jafri as a source of ideas for an alternative discourse on the nature of modernity. Indeed, proposals for alternative discourses were the logical outcomes of critical assessments of the state of the humanities and social sciences that identified Orientalism, Eurocentrism, academic dependency and other problems as defining characteristics of the various disciplines. Such critiques were made by Iranian thinkers such as thinkers and activists such as Jalal Al-e Ahmad, Seyyed Fakhroddin Shadman, Ahmad Fardid, Ali Shari'ati and others. The Iranian revolution initially created an atmosphere that was generally receptive of such critiques, thereby promoting the notion of alternative discourses or thought (*andisheh-ye digar*). It was hoped and believed that such alternatives would replace Eurocentric theories of society that Al-e Ahmad and others of his generation problematized. The desire was both to be original in theorizing and to contribute to the understanding of the conditions of our modern life. With respect to the problem of originality, Ali Shari'ati said the following:

> *The question now arises, what is the correct method? In order to learn and to know Islam, we must not imitate and make use of European methods- the naturalistic, psychological or sociological methods. We must be innovative in the choice of methods. We must of course learn the scientific methods of Europe, but we do not necessarily need to follow them.*[1]

What Shari'ati says about methods applies equally to theory and all other dimensions of the scientific process.

1-Ali Shari'ati. *Ravish-e Shenakht-e Islam*, Majmu'eh Athar 28, 1362, p.56. This quote is taken from "Approaches to the Understanding of Islam" in Ali Shari'ati, *On the Sociology of Islam*, Hamid Algar, trans., Berkeley: Mizan Press., 1979.

The problem of the imitation of Western ideas came hand in hand with self-deprecation with respect to local traditions. There was an alienation from tradition in the sense that tradition was no longer the standpoint from which the world was seen and it ceased to provide concepts that could be deployed by thinkers to explain the modern society and its pathologies.

Hamid Enayat referred to the alienation of educated Iranians from their Muslim heritage. He regarded such Iranians as victims of a widespread view that it was Iranian Islamic political and social ideas that acted as obstacles to progress. The consequence of this negative predisposition towards Islam was that there was little interest in Iranian or Islamic thought and institutions.[1] While this was probably truer of Enayat's time more than forty years ago than today, the phenomenon of alienation from heritage continues to be an obstacle to the generation of Muslim and Iranian that may enrich the systematic study of Iranian society.

The problems of imitation, *gharbzadegi* and alienation can be seen to be parts of a more general problem that defines the knowledge construction in Iran and elsewhere, that of Orientalism. Among the traits of Orientalism as listed by Enayat are:

1) It is a systematic body of knowledge about the Orient that functioned as a stratagem for colonial subjugation. As such, it cannot be expected to yield authentic knowledge of the East.[2]

1- Hamid Enayat, "The State of Social Sciences in Iran". *Middle East Studies Association Bulletin* 1, 1974: 1-12, p. 4.

2- Hamid Enayat, "The Politics of Iranology" *Iranian Studies*6(1), 1973: 2-20, p.3.

2) It is informed by the Western belief in its superiority over the East, and is guided by Western national philosophies of history which make dubious claims to universality and objectivity.[1]

3) Iranian contributions to the development of human culture are neglected. An example cited by Enayat is the relative neglect of the history of Zoroastrian influence on ancient Greek philosophy.[2]

While such critiques are generally fair and remain relevant as a reasonably accurately description of the state of knowledge in Iran, enough time has passed that we may expect thinkers to go beyond the critique to generate their own original reflections and ideas in the human sciences. The Iranian Islamic tradition is a repository of ideas that have the potential to be developed into social science theories. The works of thinkers such as Ali Shari'ati, Morteza Motahhari and Allama Jafari "suggest the prospective research scenario for the social sciences in Islamic society".[3] This, I believe, is one way we may read Allama Jafari's *Intelligible Life*. Indeed, Allama Jafari's thought offers to us a way of thinking about the relationship between Islam and the social sciences. Among those who believe that Islam should influence or inform the social sciences there are a variety of perspectives. To my mind, the perspective that is closest to the way the *qudama'* is one that locates the role of Islam in a two-fold manner as follows: (i) Muslim civilization as a source of ideas in the social sciences. Examples of such sources would be

---

1- Enayat, "The Politics of Iranology", pp. 9-10.

2- Enayat, "The Politics of Iranology", p. 10. Enayat refers to the work Fathollah Mojtaba'i as one of the few exceptions. See *"Aflatun va Nizam-eTabaqati-ye Hind va Iran:, Sukhan* 21(11): 1053-65.

3- Syed Hussein Alatas "Social Sciences", *The Oxford Encyclopedia of the Modern Islamic World*, Vol. 4, New York: Oxford University Press, 1995, pp.86-89, p. 87.

the Qur'an and the intellectual output of scholars such as Ibn Khaldun and Al-Biruni; (ii) the contribution of Islamic thought to the articulation of a modern value system that may serve as an alternative to the current dominant value systems.

The work of Allama Jafari is an example of both ways that Islam can impact on social thought. The current work specifically alludes to the question of how we ought to redefine our lives in the modern world but it does so with reference to the Qur'an. Like many philosophers and social thinkers from the eighteenth century on, Allama Jafari is concerned with the big questions of modern life which he interestingly understands in terms of the three stages of emancipation, freedom and liberty. This book is a critique of the pathology of "natural life" and an invitation to seriously consider the need to lead an "intelligible life". As such, it resonates with concerns among modern thinkers with problems such as naturalism, materialism and nihilism and can be read as a Muslim response to such or similar questions and should be considered an important contribution to modern Muslim thought.

Syed Farid al-Attas

Singapore

Sep. 2011

Bibliography

➤ *The Holy Qur'an* (2009): Translation with commentary by Tahereh Saffarzadeh, Tehran, Pars Ketab Publisher.

➤ Alatas Farid, S (2006): *"Ibn-e-Khaldun and Contemporary Sociology"*, International Sociology, Vol 21(6): 782–795

➤ Anscombe Gertrude E. M. (1958): *"Modern Moral Philosophy"*, Philosophy, 33: 1–19.

➤ Arif Seema (2007): *"Following the Footsteps of Mevlana Jalal ud Din Muhammad Rumi in the Pursuit of Knowledge"*, Transcendental Philosophy, Volume 8, pp. 57-82.

➤ Arif Seema (2007): *"The Future of the Knowledge Theory"*, Policy Perspectives, Volume, pp.

➤ Bogosian Eric (1950): *Sex, Drugs, and Rock and Roll*, New York: Harper Collins.

➤ Burckhardt Titus (1983): *Abd al-Karim Al Jili's Universal Man: Extracts translated with commentary*, Sotland: Bashara Publications.

➤ Camus Albert (1955), *The Myth of Sisyphus*, London, Vintage Publishing.

➤ Carrel Alexis (1935): *Man The Unknown*, New York and London, Harper and Brothers.

➤ Chittick William C. (2005): *The Elixir of The Gnostics: Translation of MullaSadra's (Iksir al – Arifin)*.Lahore: Suhail Academy.

➤ Freud Sigmund (1930): *Civilization and its Discontents*, The Standard Edition of the Complete Psychological Works of Sigmund Freud, Volume XXI (1927-1931): *The Future of an Illusion, Civilization and its Discontents, and Other Works*, 57-14.

➤ Freud Sigmund (1964): *New introductory lectures on psychoanalysis*, WW Norton & Company.

➤ Husserl Edmund (1990): *Ideen: Ideas pertaining to a pure phenomenology and to a phenomenological philosophy*, Kluwer Academic Publications.

➤ Iqbal Muhammad (1934): *Reconstruction of Religious Thought in Islam*[online]availableat:http://www.tolueislam.com/Bazm/dr Iqbal/AI_Reconstruction.htm retrieved [18-06.2002] from Tolu-e-Islam database.

➤ Lorenz Konrad (1974): *Civilized Man's Eight Deadly Sins*, London, Methuen Publisher.

➤ Oldenburg Zoe (1959): *Massacre at Montsegur*, New York: Dorset Press.

➤ Machiavelli Nicolo (1985): *The Prince*, translation: Harvey C. Mansfield, Jr, Chicago: University of Chicago Press.

➤ Mill, John Stuart (1998): *Utilitarianism*, Oxford: Oxford University Press.

➤ Naderlew Beytollah (2008): *A Critical Study of Wittgenstein's Theory of Language Games*, Tabriz, Tabriz University Press.

➤ Nasr Seyed H. & Leaman Oliver (Eds) (2001): *History of Islamic Philosophy*, New York: Routledge.

➤ Renard John (2001): *All The King's Falcons: Rumi on Prophets and Revelations*, Lahore: Sohail Academy.

➤ Rumi M. Jalalodin (1990): *Mathnavi'e Ma'navi* (Spiritual Couplets), translated, edited and glossed by Reynold A. Nicholson, London, Cambridge University Press.

➤ Rumi M. Jalalodin (1893): *Selected Poems from the Dıvani Shamsi Tabrız*, trans. R. A. Nicholson, London, Cambridge University Press.

➤ Rumi M. Jalalodin (2009): *Mystical Poems of Rumi*, trans. A. J. Arberry, Chicago, The University of Chicago Press.

➤ Russell Bertrand (1938): *Power: A New Social Analysis*, London, Allen and Unwin.

➢ Ryle J.C. (1981): *The Five English Reformers, Banner of Truth Trust,* Reprint, pp. 31-32.

➢ Sadra Mulla (1981): "*Asfar,* 9 vols." Dar Ihiya'al-Tarath al-'Arabi, Beirut.

➢ Safavi Seyed G. (2006) *The Structure of Rumi's Mathnawi,* London.

➢ Safavi Seyed, G. (2007): *"Rumi and MullaSadra on Theoretical and Practical Reason",* Transcendental Philosophy, Volume 8, pp.

➢ Schütz Alfred, & Luckmann Thomas (1980): *"The structures of the life-world* (Vol. 1)", Northwestern University Press.

➢ Sidgwick Henry (1907): *The Method of Ethics,* New York: Dover.

➢ Wilson Edward, O. (1998): *Consilience: The Unity of Knowledge,* New York: Knopf.

➢ Whitehead Alfred North (1967): *Adventures of Ideas,* New York, The Free Press.

Selected Works by Allama M. T. Jafari

- *Translation and interpretation of Nahj-ol-Balaghe* (in 27 volumes) (2000), The Allama Jafari Institute, Tehran.

- *Rumi: the Man and his Ideas, an Interpretation, Criticism and Analysis of Mathnavi'e Ma'navi* (in 15 volumes) (2002), The Allama Jafari Institute, Tehran.

- *Archaeology of Ideas: a Collection of Interviews and Dialogues* (2010), The Allama Jafari Institute, Tehran.

- *A Comparative Study of Islamic and Western Concepts of Human Rights* (2006), The Allama Jafari Institute, Tehran.

- *The Philosophy of Religion* (2008), The Institute of Islamic Culture and Thought, Tehran.

- *On the Philosophy of Science* (2002), The Allama Jafari Institute, Tehran.

- *The Conscience* (2002), The Allama Jafari Institute, Tehran.

- *Morality and Religion* (2000), The Allama Jafari Institute, Tehran.

- *The Principles of Education* (2008), The Allama Jafari Institute, Tehran.

- *Qur'an the Symbol of Intelligible Life* (2005), The Allama Jafari Institute, Tehran.

- *Aesthetics and Art from an Islamic Point of View* (2008), The Allama Jafari Institute, Tehran.

GENERAL INDEX

Due to their ubiquity in the text, some terms have not been indexed below and these include God, Life, Natural Life, Intelligible Life, Quran and human being. (This index has been prepared by Dr. Beytollah Naderlew)

PUBLISHED BOOKS

1) Positive Mysticism (English)

2) The Conscience (English)

3) Pioneer Culture to the rescue of mankind (English)

4) The mystery Of Life (English)

5) Intelligible Life (English)

TO BE PUBLISHED SOON:

1- Intelligible Life (Russian)

2- A Comparative Study of Islamic and Western Concepts of Human Rights (English & Russian & French)

3- Archaeology of Ideas, A Collection of Interviews and dialogues (English & Russian)

4- The Human Genome Project (English)

5- Aesthetics and Art in Islam (Italian & Russian)

6- Imam Hossein's prayers at the Arafat Desert (Swedish & Russian& Turkish)

7- Pursuant Culture Pioneer Culture (Russian)

8- Foundations of Education (Russian)

9- The philosophy & Aim of Life (Russian)

10- Imam Hossein(a.s) The Martyr of Human Pioneer Culture (Arabic)